SO-AIT-971

Published By
Rhea Leto Media Group, LLC
6854 Orcutt Avenue
Long Beach, California 90805
Phone: 424.250.3773
Email: rhea@rhealeto.com
www.rhealeto.com

Cover and Interior Design By
Rhea Leto Media Group, LLC
www.RheaLeto.com

ISBN: 978-0-9904727-7-3

This is a work of fiction. Names, characters, business, places, events and incidents are either the products of the author's imagination or used in a fictitious manner. Any resemblance to actual persons, living or dead, or actual events is purely coincidental.

For inquires, contact the publisher.

Printed and Bound in the United States of America.

Table of Contents

FIRST FOREWORD

Young people have a lot to say -- about their lives, about their families, about their communities and about the world they live in. But far too often, young people are not given the opportunity to share their voice. They are silenced, devalued and given limited recognition as academic scholars and intellectuals. This is especially true for Black and Latino males growing up in America's poor and under-resourced urban communities. This is certainly the case in Watts, a 2.12 square mile community in South Los Angeles.

As a high school principal at Alain LeRoy Locke College Prep Academy in Watts, I see first-hand how Black and Latino Boys are undervalued and held to low expectations inside and outside the classroom. I see first-hand the emotional and intellectual depreciation this treatment creates. Too frequently, I hear my boys express the belief that no one is interested in hearing what they have to say; that what they have to say is not important. They fail to realize that their lives and experiences matter! They fail to realize that their voices are priceless and have the power to transform and heal their community.

Yet, regardless of how many times I preached this message, too many of my boys didn't believe it. They were stuck in believing that the circumstances that surrounded them and the negative stereotypes perpetuated by the media about their neighborhood defined who they were and who they are. More often than I care to admit, I have heard Black and Latino boys say, "We're from Watts, no one takes us seriously out here. We're not expected to make it."

The pain and frustration of hearing these words led me to partner with CJ Miller to bring the PHABB5 writing curriculum to the Latino Male Success Alliance (MSA) advisory class in the spring of 2016. The MSA comprised of 70 Latino male students in grades 10 and 11 in three advisory classes. They are all first generation college-bound students with varying degrees of social and economic challenges, which regularly get in the way of their academic success.

Over the course of a semester, CJ taught the boys the elements of storytelling and how to use writing as a tool to share their lived experiences, to empower themselves and their community. The idea of being published authors both scared and excited the boys. The goal was for the boys to reflect on some of the experiences that have shaped who they are as young Latino males, while learning how to effectively write narrative fiction or non-fiction stories. After several submitted drafts from all the boys, 22 stories were selected to share in this short stories anthology. Each story is based on non-fiction and personal events. Some stories are funny, some are sad and others are painful. Through the process of writing, the boys learned a lot about themselves and each other. They learned that what they have to say really does matter and that someone actually cares about the ideas they produce.

As you read, *Where I'm From*, I hope that it leaves you as inspired as I am, and that you come to acknowledge the transformative power writing can have on lives of Latino boys living in one of America's toughest neighborhoods. I hope you gain a profound appreciation for the voices of young people; specifically, the voices of talented and urban Latino males. This book is the first of many to follow in the coming years. I am humbled and honored to have been a part of its creation.

I want to thank CJ for his unwavering commitment to this project and for helping our boys to stay the course to become published authors. I also want to thank Mr. Cubias, Mr. Navarro and Mr. Vega for being supportive and loving teachers throughout the process. And to the boys… I want to say, I'm proud of you! No one can ever tell you that your voice no longer matters. It will be alive in this book forever.

— Dr. James R. Marín

Principal, Alain LeRoy Locke College Prep Academy

SECOND FOREWORD

Like wild lions, hope, fear, love, pain, peace, forgiveness, and faith roam and roar in the wilderness of one's soul. It is only when the right words discover the pen of a ready writer are their voices truly heard and liberated.

This is more than an anthology of stories by twenty-two Phabb5 student authors at Alain LeRoy Locke High School. Instead they are the hieroglyphics of their hearts written on the walls of the pages within this book.

— C.J. Miller

Founder, Phabb5

ACKNOWLEDGEMENT

The Phabb5 program would like to send a very special thank you to Marco Orozco and his team at the Best Buy in Compton, CA for being our technology sponsor for the book publishing school year of 2015-2016.

1

Love Yourz

By

Kevin Esparza

"You're a bastard — just like your father was," my uncle shouted at me as I grabbed my backpack off the worn sofa to go to school.

This mangy old man had come to live with us three years ago after his girlfriend left him. He had become yet another bully in my life. Without a glance back, I left the house to start walking to school.

On my way to school, negative thoughts swirled in my mind as I spied the Burger King front booth window, filled with gang members laughing off the violence of the night before. I kept my eyes averted and tried to make myself invisible when suddenly an old G thwarted my strategy.

"Hey, son, want some weed?" he asked as he toppled towards me with his frail frame, which wreaked more of cigarette smoke than any herbal remedy.

I considered it for a minute but declined with a soft shake of my head. My feet kept walking forwards but my feelings scattered in a hundred directions. I inhaled the fresh air as I bolstered my decision; that stuff is not going to help me.

As I slowly made my way up the school stairs, I adjusted the backpack higher on my shoulder. I entered the noisy school hallway and blanked all the groupings of students — new, shy couples, contrasted with long-standing, relaxed couples; groups of gossiping girls putting the finishing touches on their hairstyles, contrasted with squads of brash boys bragging about things they wished they had done.

Another voice startled me out of my morning habit of canvassing the hall — a teacher. Is it my Math teacher? History?

"How've you been, Kevin?" he asked in a tone that did not really want an answer and certainly did not want a real answer.

Deep inside, I knew I was not doing well at all; so I ignored him and side-stepped the tall teacher. I just kept on moving through the hallway gauntlet like I did not hear anything.

The shouts, laughter, and flirting students tempered by the teachers' fruitless warnings were finally starting to drown out the repeated phrase my uncle had berated me with since he had moved in, *"You're a bastard — just like your father was."*

I did not know what to do with this constantly repeated statement from him. It was slowly but steadily eating into my mind.

I gulped a breath of stale air and stuffed these thoughts deeper into the locked box that was my psyche.

In life, a bad morning doesn't lead to a good day — and this was no exception.

I spied them a mile off — the group of kids that had designated me as their "toy" sauntered towards me, to clown on me right in my face as they grabbed my lunch.

I am not even sad about the sandwich, as I think about my uncle standing in the kitchen sizing me up for his morning onslaught on my self-esteem. My uncle had leaned his palm on the stained countertop to support his sickly body, cloaked in his threadbare green bathrobe. I had spread the thick, dry peanut butter over the Wonder bread that stuck to the thick, brown paste and ripped up with each spread.

The sugary grape jelly was already bleeding through the cheap white bread as the head clown took a huge bite from a corner, chewed a few bites of the nasty concoction, looked at me with disgust, and pounded the rest of the sandwich into a nearby trash bin.

My day was just getting worse.

The day passed before my drooping eyes as I retreated to a world of silence in my mind. I developed this skill where I can walk through a hall, sit at a desk, look around at people and things, but not really "be" there.

Once I made the mistake of getting excited about a possible field trip to the Science Museum. My mom kept pretending to forget to sign the permission slip, but I knew it was really because she didn't have the entrance ticket money. Maybe she did have the money, but she didn't want me to hope for something. Maybe she was protecting me from the danger of disappointment. After all, how would a field trip to the Science Museum really change my life?

Who was my father anyway?

The bell rang and a rush of blood re-entered my eyes as I focused in on my surroundings.

The students poured out from the school's front double doors as they made their way into their afternoons, filled with wasted time and their late nights filled with poor choices.

But I was a being, swimming upstream, away from the madness as I made my way against the crowd to break out of the dry school air to the barren, trash-strewn field behind the school.

Finally, quiet.

I liked the dust of the soccer field behind the school. As I kicked the ball into the chain link fence, a warmth in my abdomen built into a fire.

I ran to retrieve the soccer ball, kicked it, and heard the jangle of impact as the fence reverberated.

No one bothered me when I was kicking a ball.

I ran to retrieve the soccer ball, kicked it, and heard the jangle of impact as the fence reverberated.

No one was ever going to bother me again.

I ran to retrieve the soccer ball, kicked it, and heard the jangle of impact as the fence reverberated.

One day soon, I was going to take my family out the hood.

I ran to retrieve the soccer ball, kicked it, and heard the jangle of impact as the fence reverberated.

No one was ever going to stop me.

I practiced every single day until I felt out of this world.

As I walked home, I tried to hold on to the euphoria. But it weakened with each exhalation and was replaced with fear with each inhalation.

From outside the house, I heard my uncle shrieking at my grandma.

"Where's my money!?" he repeatedly stammered from his addiction-addled mind.

I imagined her cowering on the sofa where I had had my backpack sitting earlier that morning. In my mind's eye, I could see his bloodshot eyes and the black dot that swam in the white of his left eye.

As I walked up the three porch steps, I grabbed the rail as if I were the one who was sick.

I did not want to exhale my hope and power, but I had to in order just to survive to get to the next step.

I did not want to inhale that toxic world, but I had to in order to just survive to get to the next step.

Walking up the three stairs drained me as I finally opened the front door and seamlessly passed into my family's world of confusion.

I slinked passed my teetering uncle who was now ranting about my sisters and my mom. He howled that they always do this and they never do that.

I emotionally shut down like I do at school until I reached the safety of my room.

I closed the door.

Finally, quiet.

I took my ratty books and soccer gear out of my backpack.

Please, God, let everything come out okay.

My eyes darted to my quote taped to the mirror. I knew it by heart, but I still looked at it for its truth and comfort: "Every morning you have two choices: continue to sleep with your dreams, or wake up and chase them."

I was not going to sleepwalk away my life by being a gang member and selling drugs.

I would not be sitting in the Burger King front booth bragging about beating up some enemy, getting some chick high for the first time, or wearing cheap things that glittered as I reached for greasy French fries.

They were not the self-proclaimed princes and kings of this world.

They were living in delusion.

A knock startled me.

Is it my uncle?

What does it mean that I'm a bastard?

"Where were you?" my mom questioned me, through the closed door.

She did not understand why I was always late coming home from school and why I could not find the words to explain to her how I felt when I played soccer.

I slowly opened the door and peered over her shoulder to see my uncle fidgeting by the living room window, looking out the curtain at the world passing him by.

My mother lightly held my chin with her calloused hand and asked, "Are you doing drugs?"

A flair ignited in my heart and indignation spewed from my mouth. I can't believe myself but I am fully screaming at her shocked face.

I slammed the bedroom door, stomped through the living room, and pushed myself out the front door. Each step down the porch stairs rekindled my true self and my real power.

My phone in my jacket pocket vibrated with message alerts as I walked to the park at the end of the block. When I made it to the swings, I stared down a younger kid who shyly got off the rubber black swing that I had commandeered as my own.

I looked at the innumerable missed calls and increasingly hysterical texts from my mom. I felt bad, but I did not want to go home for so many reasons. Thoughts of how to kill myself filtered through my mind, but my guts spoke back to these thoughts.

I knew I did not really want to kill myself.

I deeply inhaled the dusty air of the park and it reminded me of the dusty air of the school field.

Clarity opened my mind.

I was so blessed that my family cared about me. They were mine; I was theirs.

I swung as high as possible on the swing and my stomach dropped out each time I reached for the sky. The swing buckled and twisted as I pumped my legs. I rode the turbulent swing and clenched my jaw in concentration.

I would not be a drug seller or a drug taker; I would not be an alcoholic like my uncle.

I waited at the park until that twilight between the activities of the day and the activities of the night.

I slipped into the house where everyone was now a zombie, glued to the TV set where figures just pass back and forth on the screen. I guessed my mom made macaroni and cheese for dinner. The bowls, filled with dry, yellow noodles, sat abandoned on the coffee table.

That night, I slept better than I had in years.

I woke the next day with a new mantra on my mind: "Every day is a new day."

Epilogue

My family is better since my uncle has gone to jail, where he is getting help for his addiction. Also, he cannot come to the house for the next three years; so, we can have some breathing space. Lately, I have been living life as it comes and practicing soccer every day, working my way out of the hood. Even though I have been struggling my entire life, I still plan to attend college and have a bright future of my own design.

2

Unrealistic

By

Ivan O. Correa

I was tired, but motivated. I was tired of being bullied, and I was motivated to teach these guys a lesson. They thought I was an easy target; well, they were going to be the targets today.

I walked through my neighborhood with an animalistic determination to even out the balance of power in this little dot on the map — my private hell. I hitched up my pants as the loaded gun weighed down my right pant leg where the pocket sagged with the impending violence.

I surveyed the streets, looking to see if my neighbor Jose had already slapped his wife around and left for work in his green Chevy. It was gone from his self-designated spot; but a weird car was parked in his spot. He better get out of dodge before Jose gets home or he will teach whoever a lesson.

Whose car is that blue Ford?

My lips pursed in annoyance.

And, that silver Impala?

My brow furrowed in suspicion at all the strange cars with tinted windows.

I had not told anyone about my plans for the day — not even the guy whose alleyway office was the marked place for my vengeance.

I had planned everything so perfectly and so discreetly, but my stomach started sinking as I realized what was happening.

As I walked past the Impala, I saw a uniformed officer crouched down behind the wheel with his own gun raised and pointed at me. They were like navy blue bees swarming and disarming me as they smashed my face into the pavement and wrenched my arms behind my back.

As the cop slammed the county jail door shut, I rubbed the raw, red grooves of the handcuffs. The week before my trial was interminable as thoughts of regret seeped into my mind.

Why had I let those jerks bully me? Maybe just one punch to the nose would have shocked them into leaving me alone.

Why had I stolen my mom's savings from her sock drawer to get the gun?

Why?

"All rise," the bailiff announced as the world-weary judge distractedly entered the court and ensconced himself in his chair in a gust of black sails that were his robes.

So, this guy was supposed to decide my fate?

As fate *would* have it, my trial did not go as the state-appointed attorney had promised. Because my birthday was in a week, I was convicted as an adult and sentenced to hard time at the maximum security Calipatria State Prison.

I put on my poker face as I entered the prison and went through the whole rigmarole to get from Point A (the entrance) to Point B (my cell). I just made my eyes cloudy and watched the happenings from behind a screen of safety, as I made no actual eye contact with anyone or anything.

"Ramirez," the guard said.

"Yeah, that's me," I answered in a dazed voice.

"No, that's your cellmate's name. Ramirez," he repeated.

"No, that's my last name. Your paperwork's screwed up," I said with irritation.

"Just go to your cellblock, Ramirez," the guard snidely responded.

Sure enough, another Ramirez who had the same dimple in his left cheek as I did greeted me at the cellblock.

I did not want to think about anything. Yeah, this was strange, but I was tired of being ferried around from place to place. I was home now as I plopped down on my hard mattress to get some shut-eye.

Like a cat, I kept one eye open peering at the cellmate who was combing his hair. He had the exact same side part and cowlick that I did. This was annoying.

Who was this guy?

I tried to just ignore him, but he kept trying to explain things about how the prison worked. I had to listen to him rattle off gang names, their favored acts of violence, and which spots in the yard were their territories. I had to listen to all the details about how to ingratiate myself with various guards in order to get things from the outside world without having to become the bitches of different profiteers in this joint.

Yeah, some of the things caught my ear and I began to file away certain pieces of information. At first, I got assigned to the laundry, a grotesque realm of dirty clothes and filthy sheets. I said every swear word in the book every day all day as I was scalded by hot water and steam.

That sucked and I found myself thinking that I would rather work in the kitchen where I could swipe food for myself to eat. And, according to the older Ramirez, I could use the food to barter with the other inmates. Food was a currency here. I could not deny that it was good advice and I asked him to help move me around like a pawn in this maze to get me out of the laundry and to get assigned to the kitchen.

With a full belly and a secret magazine that I got in barter for an extra helping of the mystery meat for the entire week, I relaxed on my bottom bunk. Ramirez stood by the locked cell door, watching the two guys in the cell across the divide punching each other in their cell.

"Where are you from?" he distractedly asked me.

"Inglewood," I answered.

"Me, too," he said and I could feel his eyes narrowing in concentration.

We bantered back and forth — *have you been here? Yeah, have you been there? Yeah, did you eat there? Yeah, did you watch a movie there? Yeah, did you go to that market on that street? Yeah, did you know this guy? Yeah.*

"Did you know Maria who always wears her hair in a bun and goes to church twice a week?" he asked.

I reached into my stomach to find my poker face and neatly secured it across my features.

"I don't go to church," I lamely replied.

How did this guy know my mother?

"You'd be lucky if you did. Kind woman. Knew her about eighteen years ago. She loved me even though she knew I was bad news. I loved her even though I knew she was too good for me. I heard she might've gotten pregnant. I don't know what happened. All the bad I've done in my life, at least she never got hurt. Thinking that's the only way I can sleep in this joint," he said as he climbed up into his top bunk.

I coolly lowered the edge of my magazine to see that the fight across the divide had ended, with one guy lying on the cold cement and the other guy claiming the top bunk that he had wanted since he moved into the cell.

I tossed and turned all night — I wanted to get a real reaction from my mom to see if my suspicions were correct.

Obviously, the older Ramirez had his suspicions, too. He had broached this subject on the night before the Sunday afternoon visiting hours. He and I both knew that my mother, dressed in her church clothes, would be there to see me. Yes, she was a devout woman, but everyone has secrets.

I stood in the line, waiting for my name to be called for me to be assigned a booth to talk with my mother. I had never thought of her as a woman with her own life. We had just kind of accepted this unspoken idea that I was her son and that I came from somewhere, but it was never a discussed topic. Those bullies seemed to have known something. All of their taunts seemed to make sense now and seemed to make sense of how their taunts had ignited a repressed part of my life and my identity.

"Mom," I gently intoned as she peered into my eyes. "I want you to meet my cellmate. He's a good guy. He's been looking out for me."

This Catholic woman gasped as if she were seeing a ghost.

She sat stunned, shook her head in disbelief, and clutched her purse tighter to her chest. Then, she dropped the phone, shook her head in rejection, and started to leave.

Ramirez pressed his hand to the glass and spoke into the phone.

"Maria, I never stopped loving you," he pleaded.

I believe that, just like my mother could never deny her love for me, she could not deny her love for my father.

She wilted into the hard plastic chair and picked up the phone again.

"How can this be?" she stammered.

I just turned back down the corridor and told the guard that I wanted to return to my cell. I wanted to give them privacy in this long-overdue reunion.

When the older Ramirez got back to my cell, it was like he was simultaneously drained and uplifted. I did not know whether I should start calling him dad, so I just chose to go early to my kitchen duty.

The two of us fell into a regular pattern of cellmates who had a special bond.

In the yard, we played on the same basketball team and watched each other's backs when things got sketchy. Inmates were constantly making deals with each other, guards, and people from the outside. Different gangs had whole languages of codes for certain supplies, enemies, assets, and plans of action. There was never a moment when an apple set on the right front edge of a tray did not mean that a lockdown was coming. Luckily, I got to stay behind the serving counter, but it killed me to see my dad getting kicked and roughed up during tousles with other inmates. When everything would quiet down, he would give me a nod of his head that he was okay. Sometimes blood spilled out of his nose when he nodded; once he smiled and I realized that he was going to need a few teeth replaced.

Every Thursday the meat that needed to be apportioned for the weekly meals was delivered to the walk-in freezer. I had on my slick butcher apron and pushed the cart of various low-grade meats through the empty kitchen.

I froze and affixed my poker face.

The two top rival gang leaders were standing in the walk-in clearly embroiled in some discussion. I heard the name of their mutual rival gang leader's name. They knew I heard it. I knew they knew I heard it. And, yes, they knew that I knew that they knew.

This was not good.

I just pushed the cart of meat into the walk-in and lamely said good-bye.

There was no way I was getting out of this kitchen — let alone this prison — alive.

I felt them striding towards me as I coolly slipped out the walk-in door and latched it closed behind me — I knew this would buy me just a little time and not be too aggressive.

If I could just get to the kitchen entryway, I could casually strike up a conversation with the guard.

I could hear the walk-in latch cracking open behind me.

I could hear their legs stomping towards me and feel the cold rush of air that preceded their evil intentions.

"Hey, Sam," I jovially called to the guard who was far away from me in the entryway to the kitchen.

"What?" I heard Sam's I voice calling back to me.

I was prey that was about to be swallowed whole by two predators or about to be saved by a man in blue.

Blue won that race as Sam began to question the two leaders about why they were in an off-limits area. I slipped out of the kitchen as I saw the two leaders drop Sam like a bag of potatoes. Sam's on disability now and the leaders got solitary for six months.

Their whole plans were ruined and both leaderless gangs blamed me while their own rival gang swelled in power in the prison.

But I was still in danger. It did not matter to them that I had not actually snitched on anyone.

I had disrupted a fragile balance and I needed to pay the price.

My dad pleaded with me, "Son, you gotta transfer out of this hellhole."

"I can't leave you. They'll take it out on you. They'll rip you in half and both gangs will take their revenge," I said in a blank tone and I watched the guy in the cell across the divide, beating the crap out of his new cellmate who had tried to claim the top bunk.

"Prison is no game. People are crazy in here. They don't play," my dad said as we watched the beaten loser weakly grabbing at the winner's foot that provided one last kick to the loser's forehead.

I only felt safe locked in my cell with my dad. But I still had to work in the kitchen. All the prisoners were gunning for me since each of them thought I was on the guards' side and they wanted to use my bloody corpse as a tribute to whichever gang they wanted to pledge allegiance to.

When it finally came down, all I remember is the air rushing out of my body as I doubled over in pain. I grabbed my stomach but did not even have the chance to register the pain before my head was kicked back and my stomach was exposed for another blow.

I could see my dad punching one guy and then grabbing another by his shoulder. That guy wheeled around and knocked a hard left into my dad's jaw.

"Nooo," my brain reeled as I sunk into a world of blackness.

I woke in a hospital bed. It was a strange moment where I thought I was jumping out of the bed, but then I realized that I was not physically moving at all. I was, maybe, opening one eye. What an accomplishment!

The nurse peered into my open eye and called for the doctor.

A man in a white jacket brusquely entered the room, pulled my eyelids all the way open, and shined a piercing light into my eye.

Get away from me.

The doctor heard my mental command and left the room just as quickly as he had entered.

The nurse kindly bent over me and raised a straw from a plastic hospital water pitcher to my lips.

I drank a few sips and tried to clear my parched throat.

"Where's my dad?" I asked her.

"I'm sorry, but your father didn't survive the attack. He was stabbed thirteen times trying to protect you," she gravely explained.

I drowned out her voice as she said that I had been stabbed, too, and that I was lucky to have survived such a wound and such a beating.

I did not care. Tears rolled down my broken poker face.

3

This Boy's Life: A Vignette

By

Chris Flores

My name is Jose and when I started at the Figueroa Elementary School, my older sister, who did not say much most of the time, and I were two little spoiled kids growing up in South Central Los Angeles.

My dad had won some money in a lottery. So, we moved and traveled all over Cali as we visited family and friends up and down the coast. Man, what else could I ask for! Whatever I would wish for, my dad would get for me — clothes, shoes, toys, and even entire parties!

Wow, do I remember those lavish parties full of music and laughter!

***

I grew up in South Central LA and went to Figueroa Elementary School. I remember waking up to some cold as f**k water being thrown on my face.

"Levantate, mios, porque tienes escuela," my mother said as she turned to leave my bedroom and to put the now empty glass of water on the drying rack in the kitchen.

I had been having problems wetting the bed recently and had been nicknamed "mios," or *pee boy*, by my family.

There were no more parties, or wind-up toys, or designer clothes. This Latino's life became a world of fights, violence, and horrible things.

4

Just a Dream

By

Sergio Cholico

Screech!!!

A white van came to a halt as the acrid smell of burned rubber

filled the air. I fanned the smell away from me and squeezed my eyes

shut — that was all the time they needed. The van doors swung open

and a dark figure emerged from within. He took long strides and was

suddenly grasping my arm, as I got lost in a hazy smell of

chloroform.

I thrashed in the dark's embrace and cringed at the beeping

sound — what...what?

Consciousness...beeP!...beEP!...bEEP!...BEEEEP!

"Alright! I'm up!" I said and I pounded on the alarm clock.

"Crazy dream... damn it, I'm late for the first day of high school!" I muttered to myself as I rolled out of bed and scrambled to find my black wool slippers.

I stood and strode over to my clothes that I had laid out on my desk the night before: khaki pants, charcoal polo shirt, ankle-length white socks, and even my favorite black and white polka dot panties. Yes, this was still going to be a perfect first day of school at Lock Le-Roy High School.

I threw on my clothes and raced to the kitchen, which to my surprise was empty of my brothers scarfing down whatever food they could find to stuff in their mouths.

Where were my brothers and my mom? This was too weird.

They must've left without me!

In a daze of confusion, I checked the clock as I went to the bathroom to comb my long, frizzy hair in a side part.

I can't go anywhere looking like this — it looks like a bird's nest!

I struggled to comb my unruly hair and I fretted over whether I should wait for my mom to come back or whether I should walk to school.

I checked the clock that was counting down to the school's morning bell.

Walk it was.

I snatched my backpack and slammed the metal door behind me just as the summer heat hit my face like a wave of exhaust fumes.

Glad I didn't wear a sweater.

I cracked open the rusty gate in front of my front lawn.

I left the house so fast that I did not even have time to think about my mom being upset that I had gone out on my own. But it was a bit too late for regrets because I had to get to school. And, two months of being stuck with what was left of my family had left me thinking of school as heaven.

I started to speed walk towards the direction of Locke Leroy High School when a white van sped by me, the suspension screeched and the smell of burned tire lingered the air as it came to a stop.

I glanced at the driver and noted that he was a middle-aged African-American dude with tight, dirty dreadlocks. My heart quickly matched the beating of a rock band drum as the feeling of déjà vu crept through my mind. The white van's doors swung open.

It's happening.

I started to run as fast as I could; there was nowhere to run but straight ahead. The white van quickly caught up to me and I knew I could not outrun the van and I scanned the surroundings for someone who could help me.

That white van relentlessly followed me and screeched to a halt just ahead of me. The door swung open, the guy jumped out, and grabbed me by pinching a huge chunk of my side. I knew it was over as tears sprung up into my eyes.

"Why me?" I managed to say despite the hot tears that streamed down my cheeks.

As I twisted around trying to get free of his painful grip, I could see the white cloth with chloroform on it and that face was covered with a purple bandana.

"Leave me al…" I screamed out as I felt someone pulling on my other arm.

I did not bother to look back at whoever pulled me because I saw the white van speed away and felt the pain in my side lessening to a dull throb.

"Are you okay?" asked my savior.

I turned and expected to see a police officer or a teacher, but to my surprise I saw a well-built teenager with a crooked smile had rescued me.

"Ye…yes," I managed to say as I wiped the tears from my eyes in embarrassment and noted that he was wearing our school uniform.

"You know, you're lucky. Most girls don't get away from the white van," he said with a smirk.

"Have you seen the white van before?" I asked him.

"I'll explain it as we walk to school — we're both running late," he confidently answered.

His comment pulled me to my senses as I returned to planet Earth and the fact that I was just a teenager on her way to school. We walked in silence until he broke the ice.

"My name's Ricardo, by the way. What's your name? I mean after all I did just save you," he said with a chuckle.

"Tiffany," I replied and nervously averted my gaze.

"So, about that white van — I've seen it around here for about the past two months," he added.

"And, no one tries to do anything nothing about it?"

"Well, the last girl they took came back like normal. She didn't show any signs of anything. She said they just ran tests and that they even treated her nicely!"

We were close to the school, but I wanted to get more information from him. Plus, he was kind of cute.

As we reached the school entrance, I turned to him and said, "I hope we have some classes together. I mean, I want to hear more about the white van."

"Um, if we do have the same class, try not to let people think you know me."

My blood rushed to my head as anger swelled in my heart. I balled up my fist and punched him in his right hand. The recoil hurt me but I sucked up my pain and did not show any weakness.

I was glad to see that I had hurt him as he rubbed his aching hand and said, "Relax! I'm only joking!"

I could not help but laugh.

We had to get in the line to receive our late slips. What a bore! But I ended up scanning all the students' shoes that were all either black or white — what a contrast the range of ethnicities and races of the Locke High School students.

Ricardo scanned the long line of tardy students and joked, "Looks like everyone else also encountered the "white van.""

A short, bespectacled kid with a bowl cut turned around as if he had seen a ghost and asked, "You encountered the white van?"

"Yeah. What's so special about that van anyways?" I asked as my interest continued to grow.

The kid answered, "Don't quote me on this, but they say they only go after people they believe have some supernatural powers and study them. The kidnappers dress like local gangbangers so the civilians won't know the government is behind it all."

Ricardo seemed more amused than ever and said, "So, you're trying to say Tiffany has some sort of supernatural powers?"

We were so immersed in the conversation that we were startled by the staff member's grating voice as she called for the glasses-wearing kid to offer his name and get his tardy slip.

"Name?" said the female staff member who looked too young to be a teacher since she was wearing a cute dress and flats.

"Jacob Sanchez. Ninth grade," he said timidly.

She handed him the slip, "Here, go to your right. Your name with your homeroom should be posted on the wall."

He walked away looking, looked back to me, and then was lost in the sea of students.

"Name?" asked the staff member.

"Tiffany Gonzalez," I answered.

"Tiffany, Tiffany. Why does that name ring a bell? Oh, I know. Your mom came looking for you. She was really worried. Don't worry. I'll call her to tell her you're okay," she said as she gave me the slip.

"Thanks, Miss…?" I tried to say as I struggled to read her strange name on her nametag.

"It's Ms. Stoothoff, honey," she said unceremoniously.

I cracked a smile and looked at Ricardo that was holding back his laughter.

I went off to the right in the same direction as Jacob had gone. On the wall, I saw I was assigned to Homeroom #29. I do not usually stalk people, but I checked for Ricardo's homeroom. But I could not find him because I did not know his last name.

But just as I was about to give up, he sauntered up next to me.

"What's your homeroom, Tiff?" he casually asked.

"Room 29, Rico," I said as I tried to see if he would take a nickname from me.

"Ha! It looks like you're stuck with me," he said.

We started to walk down to our Homeroom when I was flooded with the memories of my strange morning.

"Ricardo, do you think that I have some type of power? Could I be a superhuman?" I nervously asked him.

"Well, let's start by not calling whatever you might be 'superhuman.' We like to be called 'metahuman.' It sounds way better," he officiously responded.

"Did you just say 'we' are one of them?" I incredulously asked.

"Oh, look there's Homeroom 29!" he said as he knocked on the door.

I was annoyed because I wanted more information on this superhuman versus metahuman thing.

An old teacher with a wrinkled face opened the door. He was astonishingly tall — at least six feet!

"Nice to meet you. My name is Mr. Cengiz. Come in," he said as he shook our hands with his sweaty palms that belied his nervousness.

As we stepped in the classroom, we quickly realized that the students were out of control. Some were on their phones; others were singing; and others were doing an impromptu roast of a popular kid who had evidentially done plenty to be teased about.

"Let's sit in the back," Ricardo suggested.

I just followed him and no one even looked up from what they were doing as we found our own seats amid the chaos.

Suddenly, Mr. Cengiz's voice boomed over the din as he shouted, "Please! Please! Everyone, be seated!"

He said it with such authority that everyone slowly but surely complied.

"I'm your homeroom teacher, so we'll be seeing each other every single day," he stated as some students groaned in response.

"For those of you who don't remember, my name is Mr. Cengiz," he said as he wrote his name on the board.

"More like Mr.CHINgiz," someone shouted because of the teacher's abnormal chin.

The class broke into laughter as the teacher's blood rushed to his head. It was pretty obvious that he was trying not to get angry.

"Anyways, everyone arrange your chairs into a circle. We're going to get to know one another and clarify your schedules," he said optimistically.

The room broke into at least twenty-three different noises of chairs screeching, which reminded me of the white van's tires screeching.

I swallowed my fears and noted that the students had done a pretty good job following the instructions — it was a somewhat circular shape.

"It's not even a circle," said Ricardo with dismay.

"That's as good as it gets," a girl with perfectly curled hair said and flashed him a flirtatious smile.

"I'm sure they can do better. Don't you think so Tiffany?" he said to me.

"I can only hope," I said as I reveled in his attention and tried to conceal my jealousy for the girl with the perfect curls.

The teacher started to remind the students about the school rules and about the talking piece rule, which is pretty much just to RESPECT THE TALKING PIECE!

"Okay, who would like to start off with your name and what you are looking forward to this year," Mr. Cengiz asked.

The class once more went into complete silence and we looked as if we were at a funeral. But of course, that girl that flirted with Ricardo quickly raised her hand.

"My name is Maria and this year I'm looking forward to getting a cute bf!"

"Horny ass kid!" another kid with a hoodie said.

The class, including myself, broke into laughter. But she just rolled her eyes.

The teacher tried to get control of the room by shouting, "Hey!!! Have more respect! Since you want to play around, you're next."

We all looked around and realized the teacher was singling out the kid with the hoodie. The flirty girl gave the teacher a vicious stare that made the teacher uncomfortable.

But Mr. Cengiz just tried to play it off and directed his attention to the kid in the hoodie, "And take off your hoodie! How many times to I have to say this? NO HOODIES IN CLASS!"

A lot of people quickly pushed theirs off their heads.

The kid who had started the whole thing started talking, "Well, my name is Said and am looking forward to playing on the soccer team."

"What you said?" jeered another class clown.

Maria made sure to laugh extra loud. I glanced at the teacher and even he was smirking. He was about to say something when the phone rang.

He got up and limped over to answer the phone, "Hello, Room 29. Mr. Cengiz speaking."

He put the phone back on the receiver, turned to me, and said, "Tiffany, you're going home. But first tell us, what are you looking forward to this upcoming year?" he added.

"Well, y'all already know that I'm Tiffany. And, I'm looking forward to going home," I added with a flourish.

I expected at least one laugh, but not one soul even chuckled.

I shouldn't have said that. I'm so lame.

I gathered my things, walked out of the class into the hallway, and found my angry mother waiting for me.

"Mom, it's 'cus…" I feebly tried to explain.

"We'll talk about this in the car!" she said squeezing her lips tight.

We started to walk towards the car when I started to remember what had really happened that morning with the white van and the would-be kidnappers. I debated what to do as my mind considered how my mom would react to the story. She was already so over-protective — especially since my dad had died in the lab where he had worked. He had been the quintessential lab rat and would spend days, even weeks in his lab working on projects. He would almost never be home and whenever he did come around, my mom would end up prego and we would have another kid in the house nine months later.

Then, one day he just never came back. My mom cried each night and became very aggressive because she believed my dad had abandoned us for a mistress.

She started to not care for her body. It became this whole push and pull between us. I would confront her about it, which only led to her not coming out of her room for a week.

My brothers and I would be starving, and the only food we could get was from school. But suddenly everything changed. It should have been tragic news when we got the final confirmation that my dad had died in a lab explosion. Instead, it became a relief to have a resolution to the situation.

But it was not a true resolution because we never got a true confirmation that they had found his body since all the workers' bodies had been destroyed by the acid from the explosion.

As my mom and I walked away from the school, I glanced over at her clearly agitated form. I was at a loss for what to say or do.

When we climbed into our old, gray Toyota, she burst out and said, "Explain!"

Should I tell her about the white van?

Should I tell her about Ricardo?

I decided to tell half the truth and said, "I overslept and wanted to be on time for the first day of school. I tried to walk there but got lost when I tried to take a shortcut. This classmate Ricardo helped me get to school."

"You should not be so reckless. Some kid told me that a white van was seen chasing you and some guy tried to grab you!" she said with fear.

That little sh*t snitched on me.

I took a deep breath and tried to change the conversation, "So where we going?"

"Now that I picked you up, we can get the books you need for school," my mom said.

"But I don't have the booklist!" I said automatically.

"But the lady that called for you told me the booklist that you'll need in the upcoming week," she said, as she parked her car in front of the library

As I slammed the door of our car, I could not help but notice how everything was so peaceful. The library was a sanctuary of quiet while all the students were in the school. I pulled open the cold, metal and glass door for my mom as I relished the cool breeze from the air conditioning.

The library was absolutely empty and my mom made her way to the librarian's desk, where she asked, "Excuse me, where are the 9th grade Algebra 1 and History books?"

"They would be in the 'For Sale' section in the back of the library," the librarian whispered back.

As we walked to the back, something out of the corner of my eye caught my attention.

I turned to my mom and said, "I got to use the restroom. I'll catch up with you in a bit."

"Okay, hurry back," she said with a shrug.

I walked straight to the book that had called out to me — it was a thick book with yellow and black words that showed the title of *Lucid Dreaming for Dummies*. I stood on my tiptoes and grabbed the book.

This was exactly what I needed to try and understand the connection between my dream from the morning and what had happened with the white van.

It had all felt so unreal, yet so real.

That dream had saved my life. And, if all the stuff with the white van was true, then maybe the things about metahumans were true, as well. And, maybe I was a metahuman myself.

I held the precious book to my chest as I made my way to my mom. She was holding a white bag and it seemed as though she had already bought the required reading.

Damn, I thought I could slip this book in the mix.

She spied me and asked, "What's that book for?"

"Um, it's for extra credit for my homeroom class," I lied again as I felt the tension between my guilt for manipulating my mom versus my need to find out what was happening.

"Extra credit already! The year has barely started!" she said as I started sweating, thinking that she was getting dangerously close to figuring out that something truly dangerous was happening.

I snapped back at her, "I don't have anything to do at home since you don't let me go out. I'd rather read!"

I felt bad again because I was being cruel to her to get her off my back.

"Let you out? So you can just go and get pregnant with the first boy who even looks your way!" she shouted at me in a very non-library tone.

"Lower your voices!" said the librarian.

My mom and I looked at each other and just started walking towards the counter to check out the lucid dreaming book. That line about getting pregnant the first time had haunted me my whole life, since my mom had conceived me with her first boyfriend like that.

The librarian passed the book under the red scanner and asked, "Did you find what you were looking for?"

"Yes, thanks for asking," my mom said awkwardly.

She always floundered with small talk.

The librarian forced her own smile, handed us the book, and said, "It's due in three weeks. Have a nice day."

As we walked out the library, I felt the summer heat hit the side of my head even harder than last time. It even managed to lift some of my hair this time. I just wanted to go home and discover what this book had to offer. I jumped inside the car and felt the car reverberate as I slammed the door.

I wasn't in the mood to talk to my mom after what had happened so I looked outside my window the whole ride back home. On the way home, I started thinking about how Ricardo had said that he preferred to be called a metahuman. And, why else would that guy be afraid of just a teenager? Ricardo must be a metahuman that they had already tested, but he had escaped!

But what type of power could Ricardo have?

When we finally got home, I opened the driveway gate for my mom. I pushed the gate as the iron wheels screeched, which reminded me of the white van. I thought about how it could come back if what they told me was real.

I threw the book on my bed along with my backpack. I needed to change into my house clothes that I would not dare wear to school.

I squeezed into my booty shorts and slipped on my pitch black tank top.

I could hear my mom snoring all the way from the living room. She must have felt tired since she had a regular job and she was a mom. She had taken the day off from work in order to walk my brothers to school. She really did care about us.

Fears of the white van returning played over and over again in my mind. I steeled my courage and thought that the key to my safety could be found in my metahuman powers!

I settled in to read the lucid dreaming book and after about an hour, I felt like I needed to take a nap myself. But the book had already taught me about the difference between deep sleeping and lucid dreaming, which was an altered state where your body sleeps, but your mind is fully alert.

In a lucid dreaming state, the person has total control over his or her dream world!

I was intrigued about this new world and was curious to explore my potential powers. Thoughts about all the things that had happened that morning and all the mercurial things Ricardo had said filtered through my mind. It was time to descend into the belly of the beast and get some real answers.

I closed the window shades in my room and put towels and every crack where light could seep through. I felt like I was about to dunk my head under water as I prepared myself for my first conscious journey into lucid dreaming.

I positioned myself on the bed and started counting backwards as I inhaled and exhaled. I felt like I was walking down a staircase that was leading me into the very folds of my brain. My mind began to go on the journey of its own thoughts and I started to have a spectral view of the room and I became my own consciousness.

I'm looking at my sleeping body. Now, I'm in a white, cube-shaped room. It feels like a game.

Tiffany, get control. You're in control of this world. What do you want to know? What do you want to do?

The cube is spinning. Where am I going?

I see Ricardo. I must be in Ricardo's house. Look he's lifting weights. Damn, he's good looking.

Tiffany, focus! Talk to him — this is your chance.

"Ricardo?" I gently said to him and was surprised when he turned to face me.

"That was quick. It took the other girl longer," he said with a crooked smile that seemed almost wicked this time.

"What you talkin' bout? What girl? Longer for what?"

"Everything will be revealed at the right time! But I will say this — you are showing a lot of promise. You'll be able to do things you've never imagined."

"Tell me what you're hiding. I know you're a metahuman, but what power do you have and how can I use mine?"

"Ha ha ha! You're clever! Yes, I'm a metahuman, but I won't tell you anything more. You gotta learn how to use your powers on your own. Only then will you be useful."

"This does sound like you, Ricardo."

My mind is racing with all this knowledge. But it's just a dream, just a dream…

I sat up in my bed. That was more real and way better than I had expected. At the same time, I wondered if the Ricardo in my dream was just my own projected fantasy. After my first lucid experience, I realized something terrifying and thrilling. I needed to be experimented on in order to unleash my true powers.

I was going to let them capture me!

If what Ricardo said in my dream was true, then he would naturally come to rescue me and I would get to see his powers in action. I just wanted to know the truth and I did not care about the consequences.

I formulated a plan to initiate the kidnapping. I would dream about them coming to catch me after I had dropped off my brothers for school. This plan was dangerous, so I decided to leave a note for my mom in case anything unexpected happened. I wrote about everything that had happened with the premonitory dream, the actual white van, Ricardo, the lucid dreaming, and my plan to be kidnapped and experimented on. I knew it was a lot for her to handle. But if I did not come back, at least she would know that I was not crazy and everything that I wrote in the letter was true.

I licked shut the envelope and put our own address on it. In truth, I hoped that I would survive my plan, discover my latent powers, and return without her realizing anything was amiss.

A knock at my bedroom door startled me as my mother's voice asked, "I'm going to pick up your brothers. Do you wanna come?"

I panicked, stuffed the letter under my pillow, and opened the door, "Um, no thanks. I'll stay behind and finish reading this book."

I could tell by the look on her face that she was not happy about leaving me alone.

"Fine, I will be back soon," she said with a forced smile as she kissed me on the check and left.

There was really no point in reading the book anymore. I already had my plan down. As I started to ponder if I would miss my daily life while I was being experimented on, loud thumping noises increased in volume and frequency.

What is going on? Maybe mom forgot her keys.

I ran to my window to see what was happening outside.

Nooooo! This can't be! How are they already here? I'm not ready to be taken yet. I did not even start the lucid dreaming. What's happening?

I darted to my mom's room to find a safe place to hide. But the same guy with the tight, dirty dreadlocks and another stranger were quickly entering the house. The other guy, who was dressed in hood clothes, was easily twice as big as the dreadlocked one.

I crouched in my mom's room as I could hear them slam the front door and stomp throughout the house.

"Go that way," one said.

"She is not in here," said the other.

My heart was racing, but I felt caught between my inclination to call the cops and my desire to see if Ricardo would come to my rescue and reveal the extent of his powers. As they approached the last room of the house, I dropped the phone. I grabbed my mom's minibat she used to hit us with, and prepared for battle.

As the door creaked open, I closed my eyes and swung the bat full force. The recoil jarred my whole body and I inadvertently dropped the bat, which hit the floor and rolled away. When I finally opened my eyes, I saw the assailant with dreadlocks falling backwards and busting his head on impact with the white tile floor.

"You killed him!" the big guy shouted in disbelief as the floor quickly changed from white to dark red.

I fell to my knees and started crying. The dead body made me want to wretch.

"I did this?" I said as I looked back to his retreating form.

The big guy's faced turned white like he was in an Airforce One, doing the G-force training.

Nothing could prepare me for what happened next.

Suddenly, Ricardo was behind the big guy and magically pushed his hands through the big guy's chest cavity. Blood spilled out of the big guy as he writhed in agony and fell to the ground.

I gasped in horror.

Ricardo looked at me and tried to pacify me about dreadlocks' death, "No, no, no. It wasn't your fault. He should have worn a helmet."

Ricardo kicked the dying guy with a wicked laugh.

All of this was way too much for me and I just wished I had gone out with my mom.

"Why did you kill him?" I screamed at the top of my lungs.

"They were going to take you. What are you crying about? This can't be the first time you killed someone?" Ricardo said with a crooked smile.

I got up and started walking towards him. That smile that I had once liked now infuriated me. I grabbed the bat and swung full force at his face, just like I had done with the other guy — except this time I kept my eyes open.

"You monster!" I shouted.

He grabbed the bat, threw it down, and grabbed me by my neck. Everything was in hyper drive as he slammed me into the wall.

"You think I'm a monster? We're no different. You killed the dreadlocks and I killed his partner. Why are the rules different for you and for me?" Ricardo snarled. "Now, shut up. And, start cleaning up this mess."

I could feel that his anger was at a boiling point, so I decided to play along and said, "How do we clean up this mess?"

Ricardo smirked and said, "Gee, I wonder how lucid dreaming could help at a time like this?"

"Even if what you're saying is true, I can't just sleep right now!" I said in desperation

"I know; that's where I come in. I'm going to talk to you through your dream," he said with a smirk, as he balled up his fists.

I was wondering how he was going to make me sleep, as I felt the fist connect with my head, and my whole being descended into unconsciousness.

Tiffany? Tiffany?

It's me, Ricardo.

I want you to dream these bodies away or I'll be forced to kill you and your mother.

I want control of my own dream, you monster.

I see you kneeling next to the two dead bodies.

I want to make them evaporate. Yes, that's the plan. Evaporation.

Jesus, stop looking at me.

I'm not looking at you.

I don't mean you, Ricardo. I mean Jesus from the altar on the mantle.

Wait, that's right! Jesus has the power of recreation and deconstruction!

But if I carry Ricardo through this, am I giving him the power of a god?

What's happening? What am I doing? Don't rush me, Ricardo. Don't rush me. I don't know what is happening. I don't know what to do.

The strong smell of rubbing alcohol pulled me back to the real world as I opened my eyes to see the mischievous face of Ricardo looking down at me.

"Wow, that was more than I expected, Tiffany! First you call me a monster and then you give me the power of God! What a day!" he gloated.

"Just get rid of the bodies," I whispered.

He stood and helped me get to my feet. Pain struck my body from all the punches I had taken. I glanced around my body and could see the welts forming.

"Now where to start? Oh, yeah. The dead bodies," he laughed.

Ricardo put his hands in front of him and started to wave his hands in a streaming motion as a majestic flow of pure energy spread throughout the room. But I could tell it was hard for him to control such intense power. He moved the energy flow towards the dead bodies.

I watched in horror and fascination as the dreadlock guy and his big partner went through a bizarre process of aging backwards. They were in their mid-twenties, then their late teens, then their early adolescence. They kept getting smaller and smaller as they went back in time to their very infancies and into their gestational beings. They looked like curled up fish with bulging eyes; then, they looked like peanuts. Finally, they disappeared into a form so small the naked eye could no longer see them.

Using my powers as a vehicle, Ricardo had made them evaporate.

I looked to Ricardo, whose ego had swelled with arrogance.

"You can't imagine how good this feels! Let's try something else," he said with that damn smirk.

Ricardo moved towards the front door that had been broken in the battle. I winced as I followed him — God, I was all banged up by this guy, and we're not even in a relationship! But my feelings were so complex. Did I love him? He had shown me a world of such power.

When I blinked my eyes open, I saw that the front door was already magically fixed.

Ricardo seemed to sense my confusion and gently said to me, "You should come with me because they're going to send out the top dogs to retaliate against the deaths of dreadlocks and Big Guy."

"I can't. I need to…" I tried to say until he cut me off.

"Fine, just know that without me, you're not safe. And, they're going to come back for you as soon as you leave the house again," he said, just before he bent over to kiss me.

I tried to hold onto him. But when I opened my eyes, he was gone.

I was shocked by everything that had transpired and thought all the things I needed to add to my mom's letter. I walked to the hallway to check for the bodies. I was relieved to find the hallways cleared and cleaned.

Just as I sat down to add information to my mom's letter, I heard a knock at the reconstructed living room door. I ran there, knowing it had to be my mom. I was brimming with excitement and wanted to tell her about everything that had happened, but I caught myself as I remembered that I could not actually tell her anything.

I opened the door and was surprised to find my mom sobbing. She fell into my arms and I guided her into the house to sit on the couch.

"Where are my brothers?" I asked.

My mom was distraught as she said, "I don't know. The school claimed that I already picked them up earlier. But I don't know what they're talking about. They asked me if I was on drugs or something. They showed me some footage of me picking them up. It looks just like me. But I didn't pick them up. Maybe I'm losing my mind."

I tried to comfort her, but I was boiling inside. I knew this whole thing was involved with the metahuman world because they could shape shift.

"What can we do?" I asked.

"I don't f*ckin' know!" she exploded as she speed walked towards her room and locked the door shut.

I had seen all that behavior before, especially just after my dad had died. At first I was worried because I did not believe she could survive that long without food or water. But she would eventually come out of her room when she was ready.

I needed fresh air to think. I opened the door and stepped outside in the chilly afternoon air, which gave me goose bumps. I still had my booty shorts and tank top on, but I did not care. I just sat down on the stone cold cement trying to think about what to do next.

Right as I started to relax, Ricardo stumbled up my walkway. He was doubled over in pain as he gripped his stomach that was dripping blood.

"What happened?" I asked as adrenaline started pumping through my veins.

"I'll explain later. I need you to heal me!" he whimpered.

"How am I supposed to heal you? Wait, let me guess. You want me to dream of me healing you? Huh?"

"You guessed it!"

I was suspicious of this guy, who had punched me and used my powers for his own gain.

"Why can't you just heal yourself with the powers of a god I already gave you?" I asked.

"I didn't think of that," he said, as he seemed to ignite the powers and heal his body from the inside out.

When he stopped bleeding, he turned to me and said, "I'm leaving because I heard they've already sent out the top dogs. They want to absorb your god-like power. They're after me as well, since I have already absorbed it. But they don't know that it exhausts the metahuman and takes a long time to recharge."

Every time I did anything involved with these people, it was confusing and hurried.

"Are you coming with me or not?" he stammered in annoyance.

I made up my mind to join him and said, "Let me change my clothes real quick!"

I rushed inside to change to into some black denim jeans and a leather jacket. I pulled out the letter and slipped it under my mom's door. I thought that she must be sleeping and would read through it the next day. I made my way to the bathroom to grab an elastic for my hair. But I was caught off guard as I saw my mom coming out of the bathroom.

"Where are you going?" she asked.

"I thought you were in your room," I said, as I found the whole thing strange.

"Don't try to change the conversation! Where are you going?" she said in a tone that sounded like she was losing it.

"I left a note for you under your door. It explains everything."

"Tell me where you're going or you'll never see your brothers again!"

"What are you talking about?"

Suddenly, a hand jutted through my mom's chest. Blood started spilling out of her body. She seemed to stare at her own chest in amazement.

"What's happening?" she asked and looked at me expectantly.

She fell to the floor in a writhing puddle of blood and her eyes quickly lost their light.

I started sobbing. I had nothing! No mom, no dad. I kept sobbing and pulling at her bathrobe until I felt Ricardo's strong arms pulling me off her body.

I thought about how Ricardo had killed the big guy from before. I realized that he had just killed my mom.

I charged at Ricardo and screamed, "You killed my mother!"

I tried to pummel his face but it felt like I was punching metal.

"Calm down!" Ricardo calmly said to me. "She was getting in the way. Come on. Let's go."

"I'm not going anywhere with you! You just killed my mother," I hollered in pain.

"Look, I don't have time for this. We need to go. Now!" he screamed as he picked me up and threw me over his shoulder, like I was a sack of potatoes.

"Let me go. Let me go!" I screeched as I uselessly kicked and swatted at him.

I took one last look at my mom's dead body and whimpered in sadness. Ricardo lurched out the front door and nearly threw me on the sidewalk.

We were not alone.

The whole house was surrounded by the top dogs Ricardo had kept warning me about.

"It's over. We're dead," Ricardo said with an unexpected futility.

I saw the leader raise his megaphone to his mouth, "Give up, Lovers! We have you surrounded! There's nothing you can do!"

"Please, Riccardo. Don't fight back. Just let them take us!" I pleaded.

They quickly moved in and shot Ricardo with some type of gun that released thick, bright blue handcuffs. I could see Ricardo was angry as they put a black sack over our heads. They pushed us inside a van and started off on what would be a bumpy ride.

The van finally stopped. They roughly grabbed me and forced me to walk as if I were a most wanted criminal. When they finally took the black sack off my head, I realized that we were in a lab and also that Ricardo was nowhere to be found. I saw that the lab had a cold metal, upright bed. They attached my handcuffs to railings on the side of the standing bed and I positioned my feet on the small edge at the bottom.

A door finally opened and someone wearing a white robe and blue glasses entered the lab. He looked familiar.

He grabbed my chin and softly, creepily rubbed my chin and said, "It's been a while, Tiffany. You all always grow up so fast!"

"Don't touch me, you creep. What did you do with Ricardo?" I said as I tried to stay clear of his hand.

"Is that how you talk to your dad? I see your mom didn't raise you well. It's a shame," he said shaking his head.

I was shocked and shouted back at him, "You liar! My dad died in a lab explosion several years ago."

"Yeah, that's what everyone believes; but that's not what happened. I just had so my experiments to complete and a family takes up too much time. I needed to isolate myself."

"So, when we meet again after all these years, you handcuff me to a lab table and tell me that your little science experiments were more important than your family?" I fumed.

"Well, after all the trouble you've caused and this nasty outburst, I don't feel so bad about what's about to happen."

"What do you mean? What are you about to do? Leave me alone!"

"I'm taking away the life I gave you and I'm taking back the power I gave you. You were just a vessel, just a lab rat."

Thoughts swirled in my mind as I rested on the fact that I could control this situation if I could just go to sleep.

"Please, Dad. Don't kill me. I'm more useful alive!" I begged with tears running down my face.

"Nice try. But I don't need you. I just need your power that you've been keeping," he said with arrogance.

"Dad, you don't know all about my powers. I have things that I've developed on my own. I can teach you," I desperately lied.

Suddenly, I heard a smirking voice ask, "Where's your pride?"

I knew that snarky voice from anywhere. Sure enough, somehow Ricardo had found me. I screamed with joy.

My dad was shocked and said, "What? There's no way!"

My dad pressed the emergency button to call for reinforcements.

Ricardo flashed his grin on my evil father and replied, "It's useless, daddy. I took all your men out one by one."

My dad turned to Ricardo with an unexpected anger and said, "You're so cocky. You seem to forget that I created you!"

"You may have created me like I'm a Frankenstein, but I have more humanity that you. You're not going to hurt people anymore!" Ricardo shouted back.

"Ricardo, don't kill him. He's still my dad, remember?" I struggled to say.

My dad held Ricardo's attention and said, "Even though you killed my transforming metahumans, I will let that slide if you just leave. It will be just like when I killed your mom. And, you just left her to die in order to save your own skin."

Ricardo started crying, dropped to the floor, and started pounding it.

He looked up and said, "I will never forgive you."

Ricardo rushed towards my dad who, despite his age, was able to block the blows.

"Ricardo, calm down. Your time will come but first I will deal with my daughter," he said calmly as he flung Ricardo to the ground like he was a paper doll.

I was growing tired of being useless. I wanted to help, but I was handcuffed to the standing table. I knew my only weapon was dreaming.

Tiffany, sleep, sleep, sleep.

My head lolled to the side and my consciousness floated above my body. I was in the world under my control.

I used telekinesis to unlock the handcuffs and rushed at my evil dad. I wanted his body to hurt and swell with welts, but he felt just like Ricardo had. It felt like I was smashing my hand into metal.

I backed away and asked him, "Why are you so hard?"

"The truth always comes out. I'm an android; it's more convenient," he stated matter-of-factly.

"Wait, so Ricardo is an android as well?" I asked, trying to understand.

"Hell, no," my dad answered. "You think I would spend millions on a little stupid kid? No, he can just harden his blood so he can withstand blows. But he can also make his body soft and fluid like playdough."

It's all making sense now. That's how he was able to pass through the people's bodies.

"Dad, I don't want to kill you. You're all I have left! Please don't continue this!" I begged.

"You're just like your mother, who begged me not to leave," he grunted.

That was the final straw — no one insults my dead mother. I rushed him and used my telekinesis to pick up a steel rod. I guided the rod straight at that liar. But he had powers of his own. He caught the rod and turned the weapon against me. The impact sent me flying and crashing into all the lab equipment. I struggled to keep my eyes open as I saw him approaching me.

I had only one thought left. I decided to use my telekinesis to pick up his whole body. He started wobbling, and then started floating in the air. The look on his face was priceless as he knew that I had one upped him.

"You'll never win. I'll still be able to turn your brothers into my killing machines. I've been priming them for years," he snorted.

Suddenly, bullets zoomed through the whole lab.

Who was shooting at us? Were they enemies or allies?

I turned and saw the most amazing and welcome sight — my mom!

"Mom!" I shouted as I hugged her.

I could feel her body shaking as I noticed the gun in her hand.

"I thought you were dead, Mom. I saw you die," I said.

She was clasping me tight as she said, "I read your letter. Why didn't you just tell me? I could have helped you!"

My mom dropped the gun as Ricardo called to us, "Hey, look at what I found!"

We walked into another room and found my brothers sleeping in containment rooms where they were clearly being experimented on. My mom started to cry and pounded on the containment rooms' glass windows.

I held her tight and told her, "Mom, don't cry. When you wake up tomorrow, everything's going to be okay. I promise."

We effortlessly escaped from my dad's maniacal lab and returned home. That night I was the one who tucked my mom into bed and wished her sweet dreams.

I went outside to sit on the front stoop with Ricardo who asked, "Are you sure you want to do this?"

"It's the only way," I said and gripped his hand.

I kissed him hard and went back inside as fast as I could so I could not change my mind.

From my window, I watched Ricardo walk away from my house and out into the big world. I lay down on my bed and closed my eyes to enter my world of sleep. In the world of lucid dreaming, I would fix everything.

5

The Value of a Watch

By

Adan Martinez

It was pitch black. I was not sure, but I thought I was in a room in an abandoned house.

"Who are you? Why did you do this! Where are you taking me?" I screamed.

A strange laugh echoed in the darkness and then a chorus of voices yelled back, "We are getting back what we need! You are just our way of getting it!"

I had no idea why they would want to kidnap me.

What could they get from a fifteen-year-old Latino with no job and whose family could barely pay the bills? Were they my enemies? But no. I was almost absolutely sure that I had no enemies. But what about my siblings Julio and Carla? Even though they were probably one of the most annoying pair of twins in the world, they were

friendly to everyone besides me.

So I doubted that they would have enemies and I doubted that

anyone would try to get revenge on them by using me. This had to be

a random targeting where I was the unlucky quarry.

I was sweating.

This could not be real. This had to be one of those crazy dreams

where I woke up in a screaming panic. If only I could completely

restart the day, I would not be in this cell.

I would have been cautious, aware, and home.

That morning, I had woken up, showered, brushed my teeth, and

eaten. I then put on my school uniform and walked to school where I

attended all my classes. But when I was walking home, I remembered

turning left towards my house when I heard someone yell behind me.

Startled, I looked back to see what was happening and then suddenly

I found myself hitting the ground struggling to maintain

consciousness. As my eyes peered upwards, I first saw a pair of black and white shoes, tan jeans, and a dark blue hoodie that framed a face with a menacing sneer.

In my cell with a black hood over my head, I repositioned myself to sit Indian style. My hands were tied around a pole.

What did they want with me? Were they going to try to get a ransom? That might have led to my death because my family would have no money to pay them!

In truth, even darker thoughts crossed my mind. My family might have "kidnapped" me in order to extort the ransom money from wealthier relatives.

I decided to start a dialogue with whoever was out in the hallway.

I called out, "Hey, did my family take something from you guys? If they did, you might never see it again. My parents are probably the greediest people on the planet; so, if it is money that they borrowed, you people would never see it again."

I said all this with hesitation because I knew that if I told them they would never get their belongings back, they might kill me right then. I waited for a response but got nothing. I guessed that they had left.

At that moment, I kept mentally repeating, "I am going to die. There is no doubt. I am going to die."

Everything was so hot and heavy.

I lolled my head back and forth and returned to consciousness. As I wiped the drool from my cheek, which smarted from the earlier blow, I realized that I had dozed off and had been asleep for hours. It must be the next morning. A fresh wave of sadness washed over me and combined with the lingering sadness from yesterday. Tears welled up in my eyes, but I tipped my head towards the ceiling and took a deep breath.

I would not give them the satisfaction of my tears. These kidnappers were hungry for one thing and one thing only — revenge through either hurting me or getting their things back.

Who was the sly creep in the blue hoodie?

I closed my eyes and searched my mind for a mental match for him in my memory bank.

Have I seen him before?

I thought I knew his name — it was Jim. Yeah, I had met him at a convenience shop about two weeks ago when he asked me for directions. He must have been stalking me.

From the maniacal look in Blue Hoodie's eyes, I could tell that my life was in danger, especially since there was little hope that my family could or would pay the ransom.

If I wanted to live, then I needed to escape.

"WAKE UP!" someone shouted.

The command shot through my body like electricity. I was already deeply tired from burning the midnight oil to earn high grades.

How all my classmates would love to see this nerd in this situation!

"How long do you guys expect to keep me here?" I asked.

"As long as it takes," a voice responded.

"Are you going to kill me?" I asked.

No response.

A couple of minutes later, a man brusquely ripped off my blindfold. I squinted in the bright lights. I immediately tried to focus on his face, only to realize that he was wearing a black mask over his face with a black hoodie.

I stared for a while as I let my eyes focus and adjust to this new world around me.

I inhaled deeply to erase any trembling of fear in my voice and asked, "You're Jim aren't you? The man from the store last week."

The quiet was deafening.

Finally, he responded, "So, there is no point in the mask anymore."

Jim slowly reached his calloused right hand over to the left side of his face and clutched the side of the mask. My stomach tightened as I watched his slow, shameful reveal of his face. Honestly, when he pulled back the mask, it was like he was also pulling a layer of skin with it. Then I saw his deeper, more cynical face that was his true face. It was the same face that had hit me.

"You're interesting," he mused. "You're not like the others who cry, scream, and whine. You just said that your family wouldn't pay the ransom."

With that, he casually left and locked the door behind him.

I did not know what to make of everything I had just learned in the past minute. I did not know if it was good or bad.

I woke up the next day with a fire in my belly — I hated being stuck there!

He won't tell me what I want to know. He only ignores my questions. What did he mean by "others?" Has he done this before?

My mind raced in circles like a hamster on an exercise wheel. I could not think correctly as a hostage. It was weird because as a child I had often found myself thinking about what it would feel like to be a hostage; and now I was hostage thinking about what it would feel like to be free. Sometimes irony tastes bitter.

My mind jumped to another set of thoughts. The only reason I could think of for my kidnapping was that someone wanted to get back at my dad. But why had they chosen me over Julio or Carla? If they had taken either of them, my dad would have rushed to their aid.

Everyone in the family knew he loved them more than me because

they had jobs and gave him money. He viewed me as a money

vacuum because I did not want to get a job after graduating high

school. My parents viewed university as a waste of money and just

wanted me to start working and give them a portion of my salary.

I choked down the bile of resentment that was leaching upwards

from my stomach into my throat.

None of those thoughts were new and none of those thoughts

were going to help me escape. I prided myself on being smart. Well,

this was the time to drag out those smarts and get out of this hellhole.

My hands were still tied around the pole, but my legs were free. I

shimmied myself up the length of the pole to a standing position.

What's that?

My eyes darted on a glinting piece of something on the cell floor.

Was that a key? Did Jim drop a key when he was leaving?

I kicked off my shoes and used my toes to pull off my socks. I

stretched my leg as far as possible, farther than I had even imagined I could stretch my leg, and touched the key with my toe. I dragged the key closer and closer to my body and finally grasped it with my toes. I bent my right knee to lift my leg behind me and used my left hand to take the key.

I was sweating, but I held my breath as I used the key to saw through the ropes that held my hands to the pole. I exhaled and sweat poured into my eyes and burned with the tears of frustration until, finally! Freedom reigned as I released my hands and...

I opened my eyes.

I was still sitting on the ground with my hands tied.

I moaned in deep vexation — I must have been sleeping. Maybe I was delirious?

Voices. I heard voices outside the cell door.

I went silent and still as I listened. They were the voices of my hated uncle and cousin!

"Hey, Jim, stop being such a wuss. We went to you for a reason. Stop playing nice and just get on with what you're known for. Make that bookworm squirm and get that watch back. Use any means

necessary," my uncle grunted.

It all made sense — this was all about that stupid watch. My

father wore that thing like a badge of honor and never let it out of his

sight.

I do not know what came over me, but I screamed, "Tio Pancho!

That's you, isn't it?"

"So what if it is!" he yelled back.

"You aren't getting that watch back and you know why. Grandpa

knew that out of all of the family, my dad would take care of his

prized possession the best. He told me you were only going to sell it

for money to throw away at the casino."

I surprised myself because I was actually defending my dad.

"Well, you better hope I get that watch back because it's mine,"

he snarled. "I don't care what that stubborn old man said, it is mine

and not anybody else's."

I grimaced and prepared to shout back at him when I heard a door open and more footsteps. I quieted down and strained to discern what the voices were saying.

My uncle's wretched voice sang out, "Nephew, I guess your dad does love you!"

Thoughts raced through my mind as my eyes darted around in confusion.

Was my dad there to save me?

Interminable hours passed as I studied every indentation on the walls and the floor.

I wanted someone to talk to; I wanted to be left alone.

I wanted my dad to come and rescue me; I wanted my dad as far away from me as possible.

I wanted to breathe fresh air; I wanted to be locked up in a safe room where no one could ever kidnap me again.

The door creaked open as all my thoughts scurried out of my mind.

In what seemed like one motion, Jim strode across the floor, grabbed my upper arm, and roughly raised me to my feet.

"Am I free?" I asked.

"Possibly," he answered.

What a perfect response! It seemed like he knew as much about my family as I did!

Who was selling me out? Were any of them going to save me?

Jim headed for the door and gestured for me to follow him.

"Where are you taking me?" I asked.

"To another room. Look, your uncle and cousin are dumb people. I didn't know they made me kidnap you because of some dumb watch they never got," he replied.

I followed Jim through the hallway as I kept one eye on him and one eye on alert for my uncle or cousin.

"You know, it's not just a watch. My grandfather cherished that watch and it symbolized all his dreams and hard work. When he gave it to my father, my uncle took it as a slap in the face. It's been a source of contention for years in my family," I revealed.

"I know it's not just about the watch," Jim quietly added. "I am getting you out of here," Jim said as he continued forward through a maze of rooms and hallways.

Even under all this stress, I found myself thinking about Jim.

Who was this guy? How had he gotten into this line of work? Had he really tortured people before? How many people had he kidnapped? Who were his parents?

I stopped the hamster running around the wheel and focused my thoughts on the task at hand.

We stopped in front of a large door, and Jim turned to me and handed me a key as he said, "Through that door is your freedom. Your dad said he would hand over the watch in return for your safety. I am going to take you home; but first I have to go do something. Take this key and meet me outside in the blue car."

Jim walked back down the hallway and I pushed open the door to inhale my first breath of freedom.

I blinked in the overwhelming sunlight and told my brain to look for a blue car. My eyes finally rested on a blue Chevy that held... my

Dad! I saw my dad sitting in the car! So many emotions rushed into my heart and choked my voice. I felt that this moment proved that my dad really did love me.

But my dad did not see me. He was looking at someone behind the building's side.

"Where is my son?" my dad yelled to this person.

"Give me the watch and he will be brought back to you," my avaricious uncle sputtered as he came into full view.

So, the fight was still on.

"Don't do it, Dad. I'm okay!" I yelled so loud that it scared them both.

I could see Jim sneaking up behind my distracted uncle who was barreling towards me. I began to run towards my dad's blue car as Jim tackled my uncle and began punching his miserable face.

He deserved what he got.

On the drive home, my dad and I barely exchanged a word. My eyes could not help but fixate on the watch on my dad's left wrist as he gripped the steering wheel. We stopped at a convenience shop where I got cold water and a gross hot dog. I did not even care. I was famished.

My dad stopped at the police station where we both gave statements. When we got home, the police called my dad to say that my uncle, cousin, and Jim had all been arrested.

Epilogue

Eventually, my uncle was sentenced to twenty years in jail and my cousin to five years. Jim got only three years because he had helped me escape and helped the police track down my uncle and cousin.

I felt safer once all three of them were in jail and my whole family became closer because of this situation. Now every time I see the watch, I do not think about the negative times of the past. Instead, I think of the heroic and selfless love that my dad showed to me. He has already told me that he plans to pass the watch on to me when I am older. I am happy about that; but in reality, I view myself as just a caretaker of the watch that I will someday pass on to my own child as a reminder to myself to be as a great a dad as my dad has become for me.

6

UNKNOWN

By

Gustavo Rodriguez

"Your son won't be able to walk or play soccer ever again," the doctor blankly told my mom as I pretended to sleep in my hospital room. I fluttered my eyelids ever so slightly so I could steal a glance at the doctor who peered into his chart, flipping through the pages. My mom furrowed her brow and glanced at me as I shuttered my eyes closed again.

Who am I? Am I this paralyzed body lying on a hospital bed?

I am Gustavo Alejandro Rodriguez and I was born on March 1, 1999 in South Central, LA where I was raised in a family of eight. I have two younger brothers named Juan and Joshua and four older siblings named Oracio, Cathy, Emilio, and Santiago.

My childhood was filled with love and was flawless until that fateful day when my life completely flipped upside down.

I was only fifteen.

It was 10 am on a Saturday, and I did not have a ride to work because my boss had forgotten to pick me up.

"Boom, are you going to come pick me up, bro?" I intoned over the phone.

"Aww, sh*t, I forgot, bro. Can you come on your bike? I'll take you home after," he asked with a guilty tone.

I could see him stretching out his back and running his hands through his hair as he talked over the phone.

I was not happy, but I had no other option. I scarfed down the last bites of a chicken tamale and washed it down with a swig of 7Up.

"Yeah, I can do that. I'll see you in forty-five minutes. Bye," I quickly said through the line and I hung up the phone.

I darted to my room, grabbed my red Fixie single-speed bike, which is called an UNKNOWN, and zoomed out of the driveway, down the congested San Pedro to the chaotic Imperial.

Looking back, it makes me sick just thinking about the dramatic irony of the bike being called UNKNOWN — like Fate knew something that I did not and was having a laugh at the unseen audience at my expense.

But in my gut, I knew something terrible was going to happen.

But I just peddled on toward my fate.

I do not know why I did not just call in sick and blame my boss for not picking me up. I just pedaled the bike through time and space towards my destiny.

As I weaved in and out of traffic, suddenly, a stench rose to my nose and coated my tongue. The stench of death steamed from the carcass of a dead dog lying on its side just across the road's yellow line next to the dust-covered bushes lining the road. Its eyes were black and closed, but its mouth had blood matting its fur and its graying tongue rippled on the hot concrete.

Sorry, old fella.

I peddled on towards my own destiny.

As I neared Van Ness, I noticed a car parked illegally on the street and took a deep breath as I pushed through my thighs to power past the vehicle.

I heard a loud noise.

I never merged back into the bike lane.

I opened my eyes and did not see the road in front of me, but the sky above me.

I was not able to look down and see my shoes on my feet peddling my bike.

For some reason, my shoes were all the way across the street.

I am sure that I tried to get up; my mind kept telling my body to get up.

After all, I had to get to work.

But all of that would have to wait. I just needed to take a rest there on the concrete. That is what all the strangers surrounding me and blocking my view of the sky kept repeating. I was too tired anyway. I closed my eyes and heard a wailing sound that kept getting louder and louder.

"Tavo, hijo, estás bien?" my dad's voice broke through my tiredness. I begged my father to forgive me for not listening to him about the dangers of biking to work. The EMT's strong arms lifted my still frame into the back of the vehicle as my brother caught the door before the EMT could close it. Over the length of my body, I could see his arm grab the inside handle as he pulled himself into the cab with one powerful step up with his leg.

How were my dad and brother with me on my bike ride to work?

Everything was so strange.

"Do you want me to call anyone for you?" my brother asked.

"Yeah, bro. Please, call Brenda," I uttered.

When he got Brenda, my girlfriend at the time, on the phone, she cried so much that she could not actually speak to me.

It was probably for the best because my mouth was so dry. I opened and closed my mouth like a dying fish.

"Water," I whispered.

"Sorry, but you're going into surgery the second we get to the hospital," the EMT proficiently answered as he tucked another blanket around my cylindrical body.

I could not turn my head because of the orange brace holding my neck and head straight. I strained my eyeballs as far as possible to catch my brother's attention.

The blue sky was gone and replaced by fluorescent lights as I was torpedoed through a maze and wheeled through many sets of swinging doors.

Suddenly, pain scorched my nerves as the doctors lifted my body from the gurney to the X-ray table. I heard the thud of my own body on the metal bed.

Then, I heard the beeping of a heart monitor and opened my eyes to focus on the doctor holding up the black X-ray film. I blinked and realized I was now in a surgery room.

How did I get here? What time is it?

"Your vertebrae are shattered," the doctor explained as he pointed to a cloudy place on the X-ray.

My mind floated above my body to watch someone place a mask over my nose and mouth. It looked just like a scene from a movie.

"Hijo, hijo…," my sister-in-law whispered. "Estás bien? Abre los ojos."

"Hi, Tavo," I said with a dry, cracked voice.

I could not see my body, but I could see tubes running from my limbs to various bags of liquids hanging on a metal rack. I panned the room as I recognized each of my visiting family members. My blood felt sluggish and black in my turgid veins. Inside my body, I could feel the outline of my stomach.

Everything was disgusting.

I threw up. I threw up all over my dad.

I recognized the chicken tamale and 7Up from before my bike ride, before the accident, before my accident.

My new life had started — I stayed in one position as the Earth turned in its own sphere, as it orbited around the sun. I watched the patterns of the sunbeams stretch in one direction in the morning and slowly change to stretch in the other direction in the afternoon. The

Earth, the sun, and I repeated our routines day after day. I watched long hours of boring TV as chicken dried into plastic and ice cream melted into sticky water.

I survived on Jell-O as people on the "Maury Show" screamed about paternity test results, on Trumoo protein shakes as people on the "Price is Right" screamed about new washer and dryer sets, on chocolate milk as people on "Judge Judy" screamed about renter damage as I watched the sunbeams slowly, methodically changing positions.

I peed in a bottle and took medicine that stopped my body from making the dreaded Number 2. Morphine became my new friend who helped me drift into a sleep where I did not ride my bike to work that day, where I could still make that basketball dunk, where I could still help my mom with the dishes.

The day after my surgery, my best friend Juan Diaz showed up to visit me for about an hour. We spoke about how the incident happened and he couldn't believe it. After he left, a barrage of people came to see me — my entire church congregation, my aunt, my cousin...

I ended up with a high fever and just found myself begging the nurse for my friend morphine and then drifting off into my world of sleep.

I was flying in my dreams when I felt my mom's hand rub my forehead and her fingers run through my hair brushing it away from my face.

She asked, "Como sigues mi hijo?"

I wanted to answer her, but as I tried to speak no energy came to my throat or mouth. All I could do was moan. My mom began to tell me how much she loved me and I began to cry because I felt guilty because my parents had always warned me "No uses la bicicleta porque algo malo te puede pasar."

But I never listened.

In those interminable hospital hours, my mind played through all those times I had been riding my bike and had zoomed around parked cars, crossed lanes, and every other risky move I had made on my Fixie UNKNOWN.

Although visitors exhausted me, alone time exhausted me as well. Whenever no one was in my room, I would just stare at the ceiling and cry.

I repeatedly asked myself, "Why couldn't this happen to someone else?"

But then I would feel guilty that someone else would have to suffer this pain. I would cry all day long as I my mind moved closer and closer to the idea that this situation was my own fault through my own heedlessness.

The following day, my now ex-girlfriend Brenda, her mother, and my mom came to see me. My ex hugged and squeezed me, which made me cry. She cried, too, and tried to assure me that everything was going to be all right.

Her mom said, "No llores, Gustavo. Vas a estar bien. No te preocupes."

I couldn't do anything, but cry more.

Her mom continued, "Bueno yo ya me tengo que ir, pero aqui te dejo la Brenda todo el dia."

I wiped my tears away and said, "Ok, gracias por viniendo."

The mothers left and Brenda and I were left alone in the room where we just watched the TV as we awkwardly tried to relate to each other in this new world.

Out of nowhere, Brenda remarked, "You know, that was the first time I've seen you cry. You always told me that you don't like crying."

I looked at her and said, "I know, but I just couldn't hold the tears in. I had to let out all my emotions."

She said, "I know. Just know that whatever you need, I'm always going to be here for you."

I smiled and added, "So am I."

Brenda left, and I was alone again.

The next day, Juan Diaz's girlfriend came to visit. She didn't stay for long.

A boy that used to be my friend came to see me as well. I was happy that he came to see me.

The day after that, no one came to see me but my own family.

That night, I ate as much as I could to strengthen my body for another surgery.

When it was time for the 7 am surgery, my mom and sister were there. I was wheeled to a room where the nurses put a hair net on my head. I kept falling asleep and my sister would wake me up by sticking her finger up my mouth, which angered and annoyed me.

Finally, just as my drowsy head lolled again to the side, she did it again and I lost my cool and shouted, "STOP!!!!!!!!"

The whole room got real quiet.

I don't remember anything after that until I woke up in my hospital room. My mind told me that I had survived my second surgery, and my parents were in my room waiting for me to rouse from the anesthesia.

I rolled back and forth on my bed as I struggled to return to consciousness, but I felt cold and wet.

I asked my parents, "Ma, Pa, porque estoy mojado?"

They got up, pulled back the blankets, and my mom said, "Es pee pee."

She pointed at my private parts and, in her beginning English, turned to the nurse and said, "Excuse me. He needs new pants."

The nurse looked over and brought a change of clothes for me and my parents helped the nurse change me. The surgery had so debilitated my body that I felt like a floppy puppet without a skeleton as they took my limbs outside of the soiled clothes and then put them inside the clean clothes. It reminded me of the time I had struggled to put a sweater on my fussy young cousin who refused to put her arms through the sleeves and shook her head back and forth as I begged her to pop her head through the neck hole. My clothing change was the exact opposite — it was quiet, methodical, and passive.

Everything was foggy and I didn't really know where I was. It was surreal.

In good news, I was assigned to a new room where I had a better view of the city and could watch all the movies I wanted on the TV.

This change of scenery had a positive impact on my recovery, as I felt more aware of my surroundings. My mind became clearer as I was able to identify who I was and where I was.

As I discovered my new, twisted body, I realized I had some type of cloth wrapped around my thigh — it was acting as a scab on my thigh to cover a huge, missing piece of skin. My nurse explained that the surgeries had been skin grafts to replace the missing skin because it was too large of an injury for my own body to regrow that much skin.

Every day at 7 pm, my nurse would put a heat lamp on my thigh to make it heal quicker. It burned, but I knew it was for my own good. I would clench my teeth and pray to be discharged from the hospital as soon as possible. I would tell the skin to grow.

Grow! Grow! Grow!

I became increasingly agitated by all the stagnant, hospital hours.

Throughout the week, I had three different nurses. On Tuesday, a brusque African-American nurse roughly changed my bandages and generally mistreated me. I was glad that on Wednesday I had a

German nurse who kindly cared for me. Luckily, on Thursday and Friday I had a third nurse who also kindly cared for me.

On Thursday, I awoke and brushed my teeth in bed. With each stroke of my toothbrush, I could feel my agitation rising. I had to get out of this claustrophobic room. I went to the bathroom and then ate my stale hospital food. With each sip of the chocolate milk, I could feel my unrest churning. I had to get out of this depressing hospital.

When my nurse brought the heat lamp to heal my thigh's scar, she asked, "Hey, how are you? Do you need anything?"

I dropped my head and cried in frustration.

She hugged me and said, "Oh, no, what's wrong, mi hijo. Don't cry."

As salty tears ran down my face, I said, "I want to go home. I don't want to be here anymore."

My nurse took a deep breath and responded, "Don't worry. You've just got to withstand one more day — Friday — and then you'll leave on Saturday."

That encouraged me a bit but then I was reminded of my ex-girlfriend Brenda's quinceañera.

I did not want to go to the party; I wanted to be left alone.

Fortunately, mom came to the hospital that Thursday afternoon and told me that they were going to release me that day. I was so relieved that I was leaving that day.

While I was lying down on my bed, I took my phone and went on Snapchat. I saw my ex-girlfriend's Snapchat story, which showed how much fun she and her friends were having. They were gleefully shopping, laughing, and running around.

I immediately began to cry.

My mom noticed and asked, "Que tienes, mi amor?"

With tears rushing down my face, I said, "Ma, quiero ir al party. Quiero que me lleves después que salga del hospital."

She responded, "Okay, mi amor. Yo te llevo. No mas le tenemos que decir a tu papi."

I was taken to a room downstairs to get all the wrapping removed from my leg. This was the first time that I could see all the deep scars from the surgeries. It was overwhelming and I shouted out of fear and almost fainted. I was crying and hyperventilating. My mom tried to comfort me, but I was so distressed that her words could not reach me.

She grabbed her phone and called my dad who said to me, "Hijo, no estes llorando. Esa marka de tu pierna, se va a quitar."

After I calmed down, they rewrapped my leg and took me back to my room. My mom gave me my clothes that she had brought from home. As I exchanged my hospital clothes for regular ones, it became increasingly real to me that I was leaving the hospital and would be breathing fresh air in just a few hours. My mom went to discuss my medication with a doctor while I waited in the lobby. At first, I tried to stand using my crutches, but the pain radiated throughout my legs and back. Every nerve was on fire and my leg felt heavier and heavier. I had to sit. My breathing was hard and I could feel a warmth of sweat pulsing through my pores.

My mom returned and helped me rise up on my crutches.

Together, we walked out of the hospital — my place of pain and recovery.

My mom drove us the ten minutes to my house. The entire world had changed during my hospital stay. The signs seemed dirtier; everything was brighter; the people walked slower; their voices were louder.

At home, I went into the bathroom where I took my shirt off and looked in the mirror. I didn't recognize who I was: my bones popped out from my skin, my abdomen showed a feeble six-pack, my nappy hair surrounded my gaunt face. Surviving only on water due to depression while in the hospital had ravaged my body.

When I had returned to my room, my mom walked in and said, "Tu papi dijo que si puedes ir al party."

I inhaled deeply and said, "Okay, ma, ahorita me cambio."

I grabbed a shirt Brenda had given me for my birthday that year. I struggled to put it on myself because it was a button up and I kept putting the buttons in the wrong holes.

Epilogue

The struggles to adapt to my new life have continued as I learn to live in a wheelchair and on crutches. My family has been deeply affected by this and sometimes I feel terrible guilt that I cannot help my mother and my siblings. Sometimes I just stay at home because I cannot stand going around with people looking at my leg and making ugly faces.

I know in my heart that I cannot bear to cause any more hurt to my family and I try every day to be more independent and help where I can do something. I wish I had something more positive to say, but all I can add is that I at least hope to feel something more positive in the future. That at least is a form of hope.

7

The Walk to the Land of Immigrants

By

Oscar Espinoza

My name is Oscar and I immigrated to the United States about ten years ago in 2005. Although I have moved twice since being here, I have lived in the Watts the longest. When I was growing up, you would never find me balling up in the park or staying posted at the blocks. I always stayed inside to play video games or watch some television.

My parents were always protective — you know the deal. I was not allowed to have a life and this made me different from the other neighborhood kids. All the other kids knew each other; every other kid was in a crew or claiming a set. I did not care about all that; all I really cared about was what I was told by my parents.

"Education, with education you can go anywhere," my parents constantly repeated.

In this world, people are born free and they are entitled to pursue a life that satisfies them. But education remains the key to success for immigrants to the U.S. where their job prospects are usually limited to hard, physical work with minimum pay.

And, because this work is done off the books or at disreputable places, the immigrants might not even get their promised pay.

Not only do immigrants suffer this exploitation, many also suffer from the ongoing terrorization of the gang MS-13. This well-coordinated, heavily-armed criminal organization causes many families, such as my own, to move from their native countries to Southern California. MS-13 stands for *Mara Salvatrucha*, where *mara* means "gang" and *salvatrucha* means "Salvadoran army ant."

The number 13 relates to a powerful L.A. gang *Los Emes* whose name connects to the letter "M," which is the thirteenth letter of the alphabet.

This violent group evolved from political strife between the rich and poor in Ecuador and spread north through Central America and, now, across the entire United States and even Canada. MS-13 initially began as a guerilla group that promised to protect the people; but it has now become the same as the monster it once fought.

In order to find safety and a better life for themselves and their children, my father and mother bravely decided to leave their home and family. They left a comfortable life to cross scorching deserts and raging rivers to enter the United States.

They sacrificed their savings — most immigrants pay between $2,000 to $7,000 — and risked being turned over to U.S. immigration for a higher price on bounties for illegal immigrants.

All of these herculean efforts are just the beginning of embarking on the path to the "American Dream" in the "Great United States." Little do the parched and fleeced immigrants know, once they get to this land of plenty, the money only continues flowing out of their pockets.

Taxes? What are taxes?

What do you mean that I can't work because of my status?

What do you mean that I have to work backbreaking jobs for $5 per hour while a person who happens to born within an arbitrarily designated geographic outline gets paid three times as much as I, as he nonchalantly flips burgers?

Nobody tells the immigrants who stagger across national lines how hard it is going to be. They escape from one exploitation to suffer another one. They grind hard in factories and hotels just to make ends meet and to put a roof over their heads.

It is not funny how they had to give up what they had to be packed into a small apartment with four or more people just to get started in this supposed land of milk and honey.

While my parents established themselves in America for two years, my siblings and I remained in our native country. Aunties, uncles, and grandmas stepped in to raise us. During that time, I learned a lot about how people sometimes have to make sacrifices to help their families and themselves in the long run.

After two years, my parents finally sent for my siblings and myself. The whole journey to America that took a couple of months opened my eyes to the diversity of the world and humanity.

In crossing Guatemala and Mexico, I heard strange dialects of Spanish and ate new types of foods. It was Spanish language and it was food; but everything was different and confusing.

I felt the most culture shock when I stayed at my travel mother's house in TJ. I came to enjoy the Mexican food, but attending Catholic Church services was a new experience for me. Honestly, my time there was positive and I was sad to leave their protective embrace.

On the night we started the actual entry into the U.S., the sky was clear and the winds were calm. It seemed like a perfect night to surrender to destiny and let our futures be decided by the paths we were to take.

We said our prayers and headed towards the border. Thanks to God's work, we made it across the border and headed north. On the long drive, we passed by signs we had never seen before. We could not understand the scribbled messages and directions in this foreign language as we whizzed by them during our nocturnal ride.

We arrived at a run-down, two-story apartment where the driver gruffly said, "Get off. You're home."

Before we entered this new home, my siblings and I all looked up to the starry sky. I found myself thinking about all of these stars shining down on my loved ones and friends back in my native country and shining down on all the people who had helped us along on our journey.

As the winds whispered around the tiny apartment building, a light flickered on in the window of the first apartment on the second floor. It seemed to be calling us. Exhausted, we slowly climbed the stairs and trained our bloodshot eyes on the door ahead.

At this door — this portal to a new life — we paused, looked at each other, and slowly opened the door. The dark hallway disappeared as the warm light from the apartment flooded the corridor.

I only heard one word — "Hijos!!!" — before I was enmeshed in a pile of hugs and kisses. I remember thinking so clearly how lucky we were to see our mom and dad again.

What a time to be alive!

8

The Roll of the Dice Called Vengeance

By

Ever Luna-Marroquin

It was to be the greatest day.

I would be turning eighteen and my dad was going to be released

from jail. I did not care about the events that had led to his

incarceration — he was always good to me. When he was away, I

became the man of the house and I took care of things that needed to

be done — a man takes care of his house.

Time slugged by as I waited until it was time for me to drive to

the prison to pick him up. I was ready; I had my keys in my hand.

On the drive to the jail, I mentally practiced my stony face for

filling out the forms and my generic answers that would pacify any

questions. Nothing was going to get in the way of my dad and me driving away from that concrete maze as we felt the cool wind rushing through our hair.

My dad was dead.

That's what the guard said as he put unfamiliar death notice paperwork in front of me to sign.

A couple of weeks later, my grades were in the toilet. My teachers stopped kindly asking if I needed help on assignments as I descended from a straight "A" student to just another one of the losers who barely completes assignments.

I decided that those "losers" were my people; I dropped out of school and did every drug that came my way. I had no need for schoolbook information. I had a new life direction — I was learning to be a businessman of the streets and my new friends were my teachers for my MBA in Drugs.

It was lunchtime and I strolled to Jackie's Liquors to grab a bottle of something or other. The owner was on a short ladder adding blue letters to the sign. I surmised that the sign was going to ultimately read: "Wine 3 bottles/$10."

"Hey, Jackie," I called up to him.

"Son, why aren't you in school? You're wasting that gift of yours running these streets," he added as he gingerly stepped down from the ladder.

I followed him inside as he sloughed along on his cleft foot.

"I gotta mind to cut you off — wastin' your mind and wastin' your money," he chided.

"Old man, I got money to burn. People will always want what I sell," I answered back as I gestured to the bottle of Jack Daniels behind the counter.

Without turning his face, Jackie reached back with his right arm and grabbed the one I wanted.

"You know, every day there's more and more word," he calmly said.

"Omar Correa?" I asked although I knew very well that this was the man who had killed my father. I had spent hours watching the comings and goings of Correa's rival gang and had put lots of two and twos together.

Jackie nodded and asked, "What are you going to do about it?"

I visualized my dad's gun in my hand: I could feel its cold weight as my hand gripped the hold and feel the recoil as my index finger pulled the trigger.

I just kept my mouth shut, got my change, and bid Jackie farewell. Things do not need to be explained when everybody already knows everything. The truth just bubbles below the surface waiting for its chance to burst into reality.

As I walked out from under Jackie's unfinished sign, I felt the deep truth that Correa and I had unfinished business. And, after all, I was a businessman now.

As I swigged down a few mouthfuls of JD, my body relaxed at the fire of its sting. Why not let tonight be the night? I'd already been canvasing Correa's house and had spotted a discreet back entrance.

Yeah, that'd do the trick.

Resolve burned in my belly as I dropped by my house to grab my slim Jim and my dad's gun.

Yeah, I'd learned a lot in the past weeks.

I cased my neighborhood and "borrowed" a dirty brown generic car, filled it with gas, and embarked on my journey to right a wrong.

Did Correa even know that he had eaten his last meal?

Twilight subsided into pitch blackness as shadows moved behind the drawn shades of Correa's house. I chilled in my new car and mentally practiced my movements.

Correa would be sitting smugly counting up his haul from the day. When he saw me, he would know from my face that I was my father's son and that I was there to exact revenge.

I deserved my revenge and he was going to give it to me.

Time sped to the moment of action.

I remember laughter — laughter that made me angrier and angrier as I climbed the backstairs to Correa's apartment. I gingerly twisted the doorknob that easily opened. What was all the laughter? My mind reeled with anger — I should be laughing with my dad; instead, he is a pile of ashes burned in the prison crematorium. That son of a bitch — I kicked open the door to a bedroom and that laughing stopped and screaming started.

It was just what I wanted to hear.

My eyes were brightly open; my eyes were blinking out of control. I pulled that trigger for so many reasons as Correa's wife cowered with her hands in front of her face as her son pushed her down, blocked her body, and took the bullet.

It was not exactly what I had expected.

I was not supposed to care about anything that Correa loved. I do not know why I went over and pulled the kid's body off his shaking mom whose face was going through this slow motion of fear, shock, and horror.

Her kid's eyes were wide open.

I backed my way out of the room, stumbled down the stairs, and slid into the front seat of the sh*t brown car. Somehow, the kid's blood seemed to be everywhere — the hotwired wires, the steering wheel, the gear shift...

I pulled into a Burger King to wash my hands.

Why were people staring at me?

I went into the bathroom and pumped the slimy pink soap into the palms of my hands. I wish I had not already read *Macbeth* before ending my academic career.

Maybe I should have gone to a McDonald's to wash out this damned spot?

The cops were waiting for me outside the Burger King. I was pushed and pulled through the circus trial and sentenced to life in prison without parole. Some days I think it was worth it; other days, I have a different opinion.

9

A New Life Interrupted by the Past

By

Anthony Hernandez

It never seemed to amaze me at how normal we appeared from the outside. I was just a regular teenager picking up his little sister from school on a foggy day. Little did I know that as the raindrops hit my cheek, that these were the last moments of normalcy we were going to have for quite a while.

The past was returning to shake up our world.

My father's drug lord days in Cuba were always nipping at our heels and the memories of my dead mother, murdered in cross-fire during an assassination attempt on my dad, were the things that pressed on everyone's minds but were never spoken of.

We had supposedly made a new life here in Watts, California. My dad had promised to stop selling drugs and become a legal businessman. I was a top student and was working on applying to universities.

"Bro, how was your day?" my sweet sister asked as she jumped into the passenger seat of my car.

"Nothing special. I met with the guidance counselor about UCLA," I offered as we pulled out of the pick-up zone.

As she pulled on her seatbelt, she dropped a bombshell, "I got called to the principal's office today."

That was weird, but not the bombshell.

"When I got there," she continued, "a guy in a suit was waiting for me in the principal's office. She left the room and he asked me lots of questions… about Dad."

We both knew she did not need to add the last part. And, we both knew that I did not need to ask her what she had told him. We had both been highly trained to evasively answer these invasive questions in ways that offered no clues as to the reality behind the locked doors.

We drove home in silence and I pondered whether I should be worried or if this was just another one of the Fed's scare tactics.

The next day at school, the classroom loud speaker crackled to life as the principal called my name down to her office. I sighed with annoyance and grabbed my backpack.

"Karl, you can leave your bag. I'm sure you'll be right," said Mr. Henderson who only thought of me as a straight "A" student.

"I'll take it just in case," I called over my shoulder as I exited into the quiet hallway and propelled myself towards whoever awaited me in the principal's office.

Our stuffy, round principal grabbed a few tissues off her desk and left me alone with another faceless guy in a suit.

"Son, may I ask you a few questions?" he asked as he flipped open a small notebook.

"Sure," I shrugged my shoulders.

"Karl…"

This guy was really racking up the pet peeve points. First, "son" and now a casual "Karl"?

"…what do you know about your father's business activities?" he asked.

"Nothing much, he's a businessman. I'm a high school student. That's not my world," I nonchalantly responded.

He leaned in toward me and asked, "Well, in your world, as you put it, have you noticed anything out of the ordinary?"

I shrugged my shoulders again but my mind was flashing back to my mother's dead eyes staring at me. I hated that I always had this reaction during these "interrogations."

The Fed scanned his mini-notebook, sighed, and squinted his eyes at me.

I was starting to worry that he might be smarter than the average Fed.

"Son, I'm sorry to tell you this, but your family is under C.I.A. investigation, you family bank accounts have been frozen, and you are denied eligibility to apply for American universities," he laid the mouthful on the table.

Enraged, I sputtered at his butterface, "What? Why? What did we do? You're violating my rights!"

I wanted to sock him in his smug jaw, but I just gathered my bag and headed for the door.

***

I paced in my room and muttered to myself, "This is f*cked up!" over and over again. I cranked up the music and punched the air.

Later that night, I smelled burning chemicals coming from the basement. I gently tried to twist the doorknob, but realized it was locked. I went to my bathroom that I share with my sister and took one of her Bobby pins to pick the basement door lock. I had skills they did not teach in school.

Noxious fumes spewed out of the basement door.

But these were nothing to my fuming thoughts.

So, my dad went back to his old days and we were in danger again. I felt my mom's last embrace before she was gunned down. I was not going to let my dad ruin my family and my future.

At school the next day, I could not help thinking that all my other seventeen-year-old classmates were still like babies. They had no idea about the realities of this world.

"Hey, are you okay?" my girlfriend asked as she tugged at my sleeve.

"Yeah, I'm good," I said awkwardly.

She was so beautiful, but so naive. There was no way I could unburden my situation on her. I imagined her eyes growing large with horror and fear at even thinking about some of things that had happened in my family's history.

"Are you sure you're okay?" she repeated.

"Yes! I fine," I blurted out in agitation.

Her eyes resonated with confusion and hurt as she gathered her bags and said, "Alright, I'll leave you alone."

"Stop, please, I didn't mean it. I'm just stressed about university. I don't know if I should apply to Stanford because I don't want to be away from my sister. Come to my house and let's do homework," I pleaded and she relented.

***

The house was trashed.

My girlfriend just stood shocked in the entryway as I blanked the shredded sofa cushions and the books strewn across the living room carpet. As I ran up the stairs to check on my sister, I saw my girlfriend pull out her phone.

"Don't call 911," I said. "We're moving to a new house," I distractedly added.

"What?" she asked with a crinkled brow. "You've been robbed. What are you talking about moving...?"

Her voice trailed off into the background and I approached my sister's room where I called, "Julia, Julia, are you in there?"

There was no answer except for Julia's trashed room. Her closet doors were open and all her clothes were missing. He favorite stuffed bear was missing from her bed. Her backpack was missing. She was missing.

My phone vibrated in my pocket with a text alert that read:

"If you care about your sister, you better pick up the phone."

The phone rang and the sound reached into my chest.

"Hello?" I answered.

"Well, kid, you have something we want and we have something you want. Let's make a trade," the scrambled voice on the other end offered.

"Don't you f*cking touch her!" I warned.

"Don't worry. It's less messy if you just give us what we want and then we don't have to clean anything up. Cool headedness and cooperation are key," he added.

I was going to rip that bastard's face off.

"What cooperation? What could I possibly have that you want? Leave my sister out of this! Who the hell do you think you are?" I shouted.

"I'm the one who is changing your life with a simple phone call. The rest is up to you," he ominously added and ended the call.

"So, I guess the rumors are true?" I heard my girlfriend ask from the bedroom door.

"What?" I asked as I tried to even begin processing how to get my sister back.

I did not even have anything to bargain with the kidnappers.

"There have always been rumors about your family and your past life in Cuba. I looked up your mom's name and found out what really happened to her. It wasn't a car crash like you told me," she gently said.

It was all too much and I just accepted the fact that my past was really just an open secret and everyone, including myself, had been playing along with the fanciful idea that people like us could build a new life in America.

We went back downstairs and salvaged some of the couch cushions and made a place for us to sit. She got out her notebook and I tried to call my dad over and over again.

He never responded.

***

I knew my sister's life was in danger and I could not lose her the way I had lost my mom. This past was going to finally become the past, so help me God.

I opened my laptop and began to search my phone records and saw that the guy had called from an unlisted number. From there, I began to triangulate his call to find his location. Modern technology let us all be spies on each other!

My girl sat next to me and studied my every move. I could tell she was realizing that I was an entirely different person than she had thought I was. But she was accepting that I truly did have a dark past that required this type of knowledge and skills to survive.

There they were — an abandoned building where they were holding my sister. My mind raced about how to save her and I settled on using my dad's guns, which I knew were stored in our downstairs.

Yes, it was going to come to that.

My girl left and I tried to settle in to meditate on my plan of attack. As I lay in bed staring at the blank ceiling that had become the visual map of my attack, I was interrupted by a knock on the front door.

At first I thought it might be a branch moving in the wind, but the knocking sound repeated louder and louder. I opened the door to find my dad standing there looking like a penitent homeless man who had been severely beaten.

I wanted to hug him and care for his bruised face but a wave of anger washed over me instead.

"Son...?" he meekly said.

"Back to the old life, huh?" I spit out with fury.

"No, son. I swear it's not what you think," he said as he pushed passed me through the doorway.

I turned to look at him in his dirty clothes and said, "Oh, really? Why did they take my sister, then? Why are we back to square one? This was supposed to be a new life!"

He sat wearily on the sofa, "I just don't know what is happening. It must be someone from the past."

"Funny how your past never stays in the past," I said as I made up my mind to save my sister.

***

I went out to our garage and climbed into my Dad's 1967 Mustang Fastback — at least he provided a fast getaway car. I drove the half hour to the building where they were keeping my sister and did surveillance from the shadows. A few men with barely concealed weapons went in and out of the main door. I saw them bringing in bags of groceries and I hoped that they were bringing food to my sister. Then, later, I saw a man wearing sunglasses in the dark night — it was my dad's former right-hand man, Mario. He was clearly the head honcho here as all the burly men made way for him. I guess Mario had made himself the leader of this gang and had wanted to make sure my dad was eliminated as competition.

I knew all about the rumors of this guy, and Mario was not to be trifled with. He was said to have killed the entire family of someone who had ratted him out to the police and left the snitch alive, but paralyzed.

I had a few pistols, but these guys were trained bodyguards with a whole arsenal of weapons. Even if I managed to sneak into the building, how was I going to find my sister in the huge building?

I decided to drive home to try and formulate a new plan based on what I had seen. But I kept seeing images of my sister getting caught in a crossfire. Images of my mom falling in slow motion as the bullets stole the blood from her body flickered in an out with images of my sister falling in slow motion as bullets stole the blood from her body.

What was I going to do?

As I sat back in my garage, tears of frustration surged in my eyes.

What good was my crying going to do anybody?

Who can help me? Who can help…?

A thought rushed into my brain as I reached into my pocket for the card from Agent Karl.

I called his number and he laughed as I explained the situation.

"Why are you laughing? My sister's life is in danger! It's my dad's fault!" I sputtered in frustration.

"Kid, you got a lot to learn about this real world. I'll tell you everything later. Meet me at the building where they have your sister. Pronto," he said.

I did not know if I could trust this guy. What did he think he knew about this situation? He was not on the inside. But I had no one else to trust. My dad could not be found again and every hour my sister's life was in greater peril.

"Alright, see you there in thirty minutes," I said with resignation.

"I'll bring the cavalry," Karl said and hung up the phone.

***

I slowly rolled the Mustang to a stop in the shady spot I had used before. But I noticed I was not alone as I saw other dark cars stealthily rolling into covert positions.

A knock on my passenger window startled me as I saw the smug face of Agent Karl as he motioned for me to roll down the passenger window.

I did so but kept a sharp eye on him.

Out of my peripheral vision, I saw the undercover SWAT team members leaving their cars and making their way past various barrels and other things to hide behind. I saw one SWAT guy grab a scout's head and break his neck as he silently fell to the ground.

Things were getting real.

Agent Karl leaned into my car and said, "Hey, kid. I'm glad you called. You really helped us find this bastard and we want to get your sister out alive. We want you to come in with us so she knows that we're allies and that you're there to save her."

It was time to rock 'n roll.

I got out of the car and followed close behind Agent Karl as we made our way closer and closer to the building.

ALARMS!

CAUGHT!

A scout had noticed the body of the dead scout with the broken neck.

The SWAT team swarmed into the building and mayhem ensued. Agent Karl grabbed me by the arm and began shooting and running into the building. We finally made it inside. The gunfire was deafening as the wounded shouted in pain. Glass was breaking and shattering and cutting my bare skin as I ran through the building calling for my sister.

Agent Karl pursued a guy with an AK-47 while I ran in a direction of what looked like individual rooms — surely, my sister would be in there.

I made it into a room and shut the door.

Quiet, silence — Oh no! The enemy!

Instead of finding my sweet sister alone, I found her with Mario holding a gun to her head.

"Let her go, you freak!" I screamed. "This is between you and my dad."

"Yes, but how better to truly reach your father than through his children. You're just what I've been waiting for," Mario chuckled as he dragged my sister's weak body closer to me.

I could see she was exhausted, but I tried to rally her by sending her messages through my eyes.

We're going to get out of this situation and out of this past life!

She began to struggle harder against Mario, so he threw her to the ground. She landed with a thud and sprang back up to lunge at

Mario. I did the same as we both tore at this maniac who was ruining our lives.

"Get off me, you rats!" he exploded.

I scratched his face as my sister bit his arm.

It was all I needed as I wrestled the gun from him.

"Ha!" I said as I stepped back and aimed the gun for Mario's head.

Mario's eyes glinted at me with evil as I guided my sister to stand behind me.

"You remember your mommy? I remember her! I remember the look in her eyes when I shot her. One of the best things I ever did. Your dad tried to get out — he gave up everything that I offered him a few months ago to try and protect you. But look what it brought him and the two of you. You will never escape from your past!" he bragged.

Pure hate boiled in my veins as I cocked the gun.

"Wait, wait. Son, don't ruin your life!" Agent Karl shouted as he burst into the room.

I shook my head in wonder as all the sounds of chaos rushed back into the room. It had seemed so silent before as I was planning to take out Mario. But now, I felt the horror of this life of violence and revenge.

No, I would not be a part of this life. I pistol whipped Mario who fell to the ground in a bloody slumber.

Agent Karl waited with us in the small room until he got the call that it was all clear.

When we got outside, Agent Karl took my shivering sister and me to his car where he let us sit in the back seat as he turned up the heat. I held my sister close to me and breathed a sigh of relief.

"Where's my dad?" I asked Agent Karl, who smiled as he pulled the car out of the parking lot and got on the highway heading north.

10

Mi Vida Loca

By

Jimmy Padilla

Chapter 1

Teachers and family call me "Jimmy," but my homies call me

"Silencio." I only bring that up because I'm going to be executed in

an hour and I keep imagining these two funerals where people at each

one talk about me using the different names. It would be like they are

talking about two entirely different people. But since time is of

essence, I might as well get down to the business of telling my story.

When I was fourteen, which is already ten years ago, I was

walking home after an exhausting day in my new school in

California.

Three cholos came up to me and asked, "Where you from?"

"Mexico," I naively answered.

As I replied, I knew I had said something stupid as their facial expressions changed and one said, "No cabrón, what hood you from?!?"

I felt the heat of their hatred and anger as I became increasingly scared. I could not move. I told my lips to move and speak words; but a strange whisper was all that would come out.

Two of them grabbed my arms while the third started to pummel my face. I started to feel like a rag doll and I tasted metallic blood in my mouth. They dropped my form, which crumpled on the sidewalk where I could see the blood from my face trickle and weave into the tiny grooves in the hot cement. I wondered why I had worked so hard to get to California just to die on the sidewalk like a dog.

Suddenly, everything was cool and quiet. But I was not home. Where was I?

I felt a washcloth wiped across my nose. The blood had dried and the washcloth felt like a thousand razors scraping my skin.

"Mom, stop!" I tried to shout as only a mumble would come out of my mouth.

"Don't worry, little man," a stranger's voice said to me. "My name's Jerry and you're at my house on Florence."

"How did I get here?" I asked as I struggled to push myself to a seated position and peered at him suspiciously out of my swollen eyes.

"I found you unconscious on the sidewalk. It looks like your nose is broken. Looks like you got jumped. Your face is a mess, but your hands are clean. Didn't even get a swing back at them, huh?" he said as he continued to wipe the damp cloth across my forehead.

"Are you a weirdo?" I asked point blank.

"I don't think so," he said. "But it's true that I'm not just doing this out of kindness for you. I have a favor to ask you. I saw the logo on your shirt — you go to the same school as my little cousin," he said as he dunked the bloody cloth into a basin of water and rung it out. The blood darkened the water.

"Maybe you know him? His name is Alejandro Sanchez," he continued.

I knew exactly who that little hoodlum was — he was always getting called to the principal's office. If the school faculty members could only imagine the things he did after the bell rang every day, they would have a meltdown.

I glanced around Jerry's place, which was a humble apartment. He seemed like a genuine guy and I was too young to know what it meant to try to change someone's life for the better, so I ingenuously agreed to help with turning Alejandro's life around.

Obviously, things did not go as planned.

Chapter 2

At home, I just told my mom that I had been hit in the face during a dodge ball game. She was so distracted by rushing to make the bus for her night shift that she just accepted my lame story. Alone in the apartment, I tried to slurp down some soup with my swollen lips as I considered how to get in with Alejandro.

My chance came the very next day at school.

"I assume everyone did the homework and is ready for a pop quiz?" the eternally optimistic Math teacher announced as we filed into his second period class.

Everybody groaned, but I was excited because this was my opportunity. I sat in the seat across from Alejandro and, during the quiz, stealthily passed him a cheat sheet.

I guess my roughed up face gave me some street cred and Alejandro grabbed the cheat sheet and jotted down the answers. He coolly slipped the sheet into his front jean pocket.

At lunch, the cafeteria was as noisy as always and the food as disgusting as always. But through the din and the raucous smells, I saw Alejandro's arm waiving me over.

"Scumbag," I heard one of his crew label me as I set down my lunch tray.

"He's cool," Alejandro said to the air, and that was that. I was bona fide.

Alejandro went by the moniker "Shorty" and we fell into walking home together since we lived in the same neighborhood.

Problem was, the cholos who had jumped me patrolled the

neighborhood looking for punching bags. I had steered Alejandro

away from their territory once or twice, but I could tell he knew them.

Finally, he asked me point blank, "Did those vatos jump you?"

I just nodded in embarrassment — was he going to think I was a

loser?

"Vámanos, they ain't gonna do sh*t. And, if they do, then we'll

just deal with it, a putasos," he said with the confidence of someone

who did not leave a fight with clean knuckles.

I tried to play off my shaky hands and gripped the straps of my

backpack as I nodded to avoid talking with my shaky voice.

The clowns spotted us and chanted, "Mira! Es el cabrón que

nosotros chingado!

They did not know what hit them — but I did. It was Shorty

wreaking havoc on all three of them: a swift punch to the kidney, a

box to the ear, and a kick to the plums. It was sidewalk carnival of

pain.

While they were taking naps on the concrete, Shorty called up his crew who descended on the slumbering clowns whose faces were swelling and becoming the blue eyes and fat, red lips of their clowning trade.

One of Shorty's right-hand men opened a sweating gallon of cold water that he must have bought at a convenience store. He tossed the red lid on the triplets and passed the jug to Shorty who took a swig and spit it out on the tall leader of the gang. The leader moaned and struggled to pull himself out of his deep nap.

Shorty wickedly grinned, glanced around at his dangerously silent crew and then dumped the whole jug of water all over the clowns. They slowly pushed themselves up to their feet and stumbled as they shook their heads back and forth and tried to regain their footing.

I felt an unfamiliar joy at knowing they were in pain.

They looked like ragdolls as they bumped into each other and were pushed back into the circle center by Shorty's crew.

"Don't mess with my familia porque te voy a chingar, comprende?" Shorty said like a boss.

"Okay, okay," the leader stuttered. "I'll leave him alone. Just let us go."

"We'll let you go when we're done with you," Shorty said with a nasty grin, as his crew menacingly moved in for the final act of the sidewalk circus.

Yeah, I never saw those clowns again — I wondered if Shorty's crew had just messed up their faces too much and I could not recognize them. I never looked at jugs of water or at Shorty the same after that day.

Chapter 3

Under Shorty's wing, I was brought into his crew where I was respected and popular. I went from being a quiet church mouse to being known as "Silencio" because I could be depended on to keep quiet. I could be trusted and I was smart.

Our gang was not just about running drugs or fighting off enemies — we were our own brotherhood, an organization filled with different people who had different mindsets and skills to offer. Most importantly, we were a familia.

Just in a month, I had a new family. I learned that Shorty did not just take care of random hoodlums, but that he was a politician and a godfather of sorts. Shorty had negotiated no-conflict agreements with most of the neighborhood gangs and his jurisdiction stretched to about seven different varrios.

But the gang called Un Varrio was not too fond of us for some reason. They were chomping at the bit to start a turf war with us. Even though Shorty had wielded his power against those clowns, he aimed to prevent war, large-scale wars between our gang and others.

The leader of Un Varrio was known as "El Culebra" — ese pinche cabrón tiene una mentalidad de un idiota. We heard that he had some mission to get our familia de la calle out of the picture. He had some fixation on Shorty and me, but we watched each other's backs.

Chapter 4

I passed Jerry, who had asked me to help get Shorty on the straight and narrow, on the street one day and I looked the other way to make sure he did not recognize me. But he did not even recognize me. I guess it had been two years and I had become a man. Time flies when you are busy. Little did I know that my upcoming year was going to decimate my concept of old busy.

I was going to be running for my life by the end of it.

Shorty, some crewmembers, and I were chilling in a bar with some beers when suddenly that idiot snake El Culebra sauntered by our seats. He casually leaned over to Shorty's ear and whispered something about how Shorty's girlfriend better watch her back.

El Culebra tried to straighten back up, but Shorty's thick hand was already wrapped around the back of El's neck digging his nails into the skin around the idiot's spinal column.

"Listen up, cabrón. Touch my girl and you'll be breathing through a tube," Shorty threatened as he pushed El Culebra into an empty table.

The chairs skidded and scattered as the table wobbled and finally toppled over while El Culebra did his pathetic dance to regain his balance. His face seethed with anger and his eyes remained locked on Shorty the whole time.

Something shiny caught the light in the mirror behind the bar — Culebra had whipped out a knife.

But Shorty anticipated the idiot's move and already had his butterfly knife ready at attention. El Culebra lunged forward as Shorty dodged him and deftly grabbed the back of the idiot's right upper arm. Shorty shifted his weight and swung the idiot around and threw his body into the evil throes of his waiting crew.

Shorty regained his diplomatic air and intoned, "So, you have two choices — leave us alone or die right now."

"Okay, okay. I'll leave you alone," the idiot panted as he wrenched his arms from the crew who pushed him in the direction of the door.

When that idiot left, a calm came over the bar and Shorty acknowledged his crew with a nod of his head. Everyone went back to his beer and a buzz of conversation grew. Shorty and I remained at the bar and planned to signal the other jurisdictions about the new treaty.

But I was only half listening — a gorgeous Latina with sweet, brown eyes passed by the bar window. I do not know why, but I was so drawn to her that I felt engulfed by her beauty.

Shorty noticed and encouraged me, "Hey, go talk to her. Don't be nervous. Just go before she gets away."

Like a feral cat, I stalked her progress through the streets. She stopped at intersections and waited for the lights to change as I walked faster and faster trying to catch up to here. But the lights were not on my side and she got away.

I exhaled in frustration and made my way back to the bar to hang with my familia.

The party broke up and I rode in Shorty's car with him back to his place where we crashed on the sofas and continued chilling.

"Hey, you talk to that girl?" Shorty asked.

"No, I couldn't catch up to her," I sighed.

"Lucky for you, I know that she lives about a block from here," he nonchalantly said.

"Why the hell didn't you say something before?" I stammered in exasperation.

"Relax," he chuckled. "She lives about three doors down and her name is Andrea."

Shorty reached up and turned off the light as we both settled in to sleep on our sofas.

Shorty's snores from his sofa did not keep me awake, but my thoughts of the beautiful Andrea did. As dawn rose, I still had thoughts of this lovely girl dancing in my mind.

Chapter 5

Shorty sent messages through the grapevine that I wanted to meet Andrea and it was finally going to happen.

I was a nervous wreck as I put on layers of expensive deodorant and a fresh pair of clothes. There was just something about this girl.

The ring at the doorbell made me all the more nervous. But when I opened the door, I saw her sweet face and I somehow relaxed. It was a weird sensation that I had never had before. Other girls just made me nervous or I thought they were not worth my time.

Andrea was special.

"Do you want a drink?" I awkwardly asked her.

"Sure, I'll just have some water," she said as she sat on the sofa.

It was the beginning of a beautiful friendship.

We hung out all the time — we went to movies and parties. Whenever she was there, I felt whole; but whenever she was gone, I felt like something was missing. She made me feel warm and happy inside.

Three years after our first meeting, we were sitting on a park bench under a tree. Andrea was upset because her father wanted her to get a job at this convenience store and she did not want to work there. She wanted to focus on her studies.

"Don't worry," I comforted her. "You're so smart that you can still get good grades even if you work. Just think that you can save the money and use it for your future," I encouraged her.

Andrea turned to me and said the most beautiful thing that I have ever heard.

"I love you," she said with a rueful smile.

My heart dropped in my body and I felt like I was shaking, but I managed to tell her, "I love you, too."

We were never really boyfriend and girlfriend because we never dated. But we were something more than that. Other people seemed to fall in and out of relationships, and in and out of love. But we kept our love about our friendship. I am not such a romantic guy, but I learned how to say "I love you" in French and I would text her *Je t'aime*. It was our thing and she made me feel what no other woman ever made me feel and she did not even have to try.

Chapter 6

Andrea had a positive impact on my life in many ways. Through her innocence, I started to see how violent Shorty's world was and how it was a never-ending cycle. This led me to distance myself from Shorty and my familia in order to keep my past secret and to protect Andrea.

I did not want her to find out about all the things I had done to help Shorty nor did I want Andrea to become some pawn in that mixed-up mess.

But Shorty had been a huge part of my life. He was a mentor and a brother to me and when he called out of the blue for my help, I had to jump to his aide. Varrios were after him and it was serious.

"Hey, can you come and get me?" I heard Shorty's weakened voice on the other end of the phone.

"Brother, where are you?" I asked as I pulled on my clothes and grabbed my keys.

Sh*t had already gone down and Shorty was hiding in an alley.

I put the pedal to the metal and drove to the area near the alley where he was hiding. I then slowed the car and began casing the area for varrios. I saw several guys walking around acting casual, but they were clearly casing the area for Shorty.

This was an animal kingdom and Shorty was a weakened foe who could easily be eliminated.

I waited for the varrios to move on to another area and then I parked my car and went to the alley that Shorty said he was in. I called on my phone and heard a faint ringing sound that I followed over to a dumpster.

Was Shorty dead inside?

My heart sickened at the thought and I strengthened my resolve as I lifted the dumpster lid.

There was my hero lying on a pile of black, shiny trash bags as he groaned and held his side that was leaking blood from various stab wounds.

"Hey, Shorty. I'm going to get you out of this mess," I assured him as I called 911 for an ambulance.

The whirling cry of the ambulance was a relief as the EMTs lifted Shorty's unconscious body from the dumpster. I drove my car behind the ambulance and pushed through every yellow light to keep up with the ambulance.

On a gurney outside of the surgery room, Shorty lay waiting for the doctors to come and repair the damage from the multiple stab wounds.

"Who did this to you?" I asked.

Blood gurgled in his throat as he whispered, "The Varrios...El Culebra did this to me."

Shorty fell unconscious again as the doctors wheeled him into surgery and as I stormed out of the hospital to seek my revenge.

I got in my silver Impala and stalked the streets like a tiger tracking its prey. The weight of my Colt .45 rocked in my jacket pocket and encouraged me to believe that I could take out El Culebra.

I saw that arrogant cockroach sitting alone on the stoops of an abandoned dope house smoking a blunt — that's when I took my shot.

I leaned out the car window and fired right for his right thigh. It delivered a painful and disabling, but not mortal, introduction to what was about to come.

This was going to be fun. Again, I felt that feeling, a joy at others suffering pain.

"Augh!" El Culebra shouted in surprise as the blood squirted from the hamburger-meat exposed from his torn thigh.

I ran across the street and grabbed the limping cockroach by the back of his shirt and roughly dragged him into the alley next to the dope house.

"You think you can just stab Shorty and then smoke out! Your ass is mine!" I shouted as I put another round point black into Shorty's upper shoulder. Painful and disabling, but not mortal.

He reeled with agony and puked on the cement where he fell to his side and then rolled onto his stomach.

I then ended the life of this miserable excuse for a human being.

The next day, the town was buzzing about the death of the governor's godson — I looked at the picture in the newspaper and reeled as I saw the image of a cleaned up El Culebra.

The guy in the picture had combed hair and a neat suit on, but it was definitely El Culebra before he had met his maker.

Why had I never put two and two together and realized that El Culebra was connected to the governor? Was that why he was always getting away with things?

This was a mess — what would Andrea think if word of what I had done got out?

Word evidentially had gotten out as I saw the cops surrounding my house. I had nowhere to run or hide. They quickly arrested and sentenced me to execution.

The judge rapped the gravel and dictated, "For your crime, you are to be executed in the gas chamber on July 15, 2016. May God have mercy on your soul."

I remained stoic but loud cries of anger arose from my familia and from my family.

It was just a few days away and I whiled away my time in my cell. Members from my familia came to see me and told me about how Shorty was recovering in the hospital. Every word was about their respect for what I had done and how they would always honor me. I was proud that I had avenged my brother, but I longed to see my sweet Andrea's face.

When she finally arrived, her face was drawn and tear-stained. It was clear that she was devastated.

"Mon Ange," I said as I wished I could hold her hands in mine.

"I am not your Ange anymore," she whispered and kept her eyes looking down.

"I had to do it. Shorty's done so much for me…," I said.

Andrea tightened her lips and looked me dead in the eyes, "Yeah, he's so helpful that he dug you a grave."

I had never heard such bitterness from her.

"I thought you were different from the other guys in this town. Now, I realize you're worse. The other guys are open about what they are, but you kept everything a secret," she said accusingly.

I was at a loss because the familia had been all about boosting my ego while Andrea was telling me the hard truth. I had given up my life years ago when I had ignored the advice of Jerry and had been lured into this life of gangs, drugs, crime, and vengeance.

What had it all been worth?

"Please forgive me, mon Ange," I pleaded with her.

"You're a killer, just like all the rest," she said and turned to leave.

I was devastated and now the hours slowed to an excruciating snail's pace as I waited till my execution.

I could not touch the plate of food that was to be my last meal.

I refused to talk to the confessor — I just wanted one last look at my lovely Ange.

Everything started to happen so quickly.

They were taking away the plate of food.

The confessor was leaving in a swoop of black vestments.

The guards were guiding me down the corridor of the Dead Men Walking.

I was being strapped into a chair in a hermetically sealed room with a glass wall through which I could see the governor, El Culebra's smug compadres, and my familia.

But where was my Ange?

I did not care as they tightened the leather straps around me and pinioned my head to the upright bed. I did not want to meet my maker without one last look at my true maker, my Ange.

And there she was, tearfully sitting on the edge of her seat with her eyes fixed on mine.

Everyone else in the room faded away.

I saw her lips mouth, "Je t'aime."

My eyes blurred with the haze of the fumes.

My last thoughts were of Andrea as my lips whispered, "Je t'aime, mon Ange."

The noxious gas infiltrated my body and carried my consciousness to the other side.

11

American Life

By

Eric Martinez

When little, I loved the hot weather because my parents would drive us up to the mountains where there was a lake. I can still see the backs of my parents' heads as I sat in the back seat anticipating the feel of the cool water on my legs and listening to my parents reminiscing about their early dating years.

When we got to the lake, I would rush down to the lake.

"David," my mom would call to me, as I waded in the water. "Don't go out too far."

"He's fine," my dad would say and distract her with a fresh strawberry from our lunch basket.

But when I was a teenager, my parents did the typical American thing and got divorced.

After my parents divorced, I spent the weekdays with my mother and the weekends with my dad. It was like a strange job that I had to commute to as I shuttled from house to house, person to person. Sometimes, my mom would need my help on the weekends to do errands. I remember one time carrying a heavy lamp into the house and hearing my dad's angry, hurt voice through the telephone talking to my phone accusing her of keeping me from him. Later, he would accuse me of trying to avoid him.

It hurt me to my core; but I would just get mad instead of feeling the pain.

As our ability to communicate broke down, he resorted to lecturing me about stupid stuff and to saying that he could not trust me or to asking if I loved, whom I loved more — him or my mother.

Aside from this standard divorced-family drama, I had a pretty repetitive daily schedule — school, practice, home. I would have liked to spend more time with friends. But my mother always said it was too late and that she wanted me to stay home so she did not worry about my safety. I used to have a whole range of emotions during these conversations — frustration, anger, disbelief...

But then I realized both the conversations and the emotions were futile, and I just gave up asking to go out to meet my friends.

It was the opposite with my father, who seemed to have a restless soul like me. We would always go out to the swap meet. And, it did not matter how many times my father would hit me or pull my ear, I still got lost in my own thoughts and would get separated from him.

At his simple apartment, I watched his friends come and go. I was able to have my own school friends over in the afternoons. I liked this. My best friends were named Jesus and Aneta. We had a tight bond because we supported each other through a lot of different problems with our families and encouraged each other's hopes for the future.

Once we had a huge fight and we almost lost our friendship. But we came back together and this experience solidified our bonds and we became even stronger friends than before.

Jesus was like a brother to me and he helped me laugh about even the silliest of things. Once he made fun of this ridiculous chair and we were choking with laughter. It still makes me smile to think about that afternoon.

I loved chilling with Jesus and my other friend David when we would go to the park and talk smack to each other. Our favorite thing to do was play competitive videogames. Our other friend Bryan was a hardcore gamer who really knew how to push the limits.

I do not know exactly how everything changed. My mind repeats every step of the timeline. But it still seems like a mystery to me.

It was a regular Tuesday and I was hanging out with my friends as I waited for my mother to pick me up after school. She had already told me that she wanted to go downtown to pay the phone bill. I did not mind — I always liked to drive through the city center.

Everything seemed normal as my mom finished paying the twenty-dollar bill until this guy with a mask appeared out of thin air. I could only watch what was happening in shock. My mom and I grabbed onto each other as we both hit the deck. I craned my neck around to see the other customers' terrified faces as we all lay on the dirty, cold floor.

"Hey, you can't do this. I'm calling the c..," an employee shouted as the robber cut him off by slamming his body into a glass desk that shattered into a million dangerous diamonds.

I was a helpless child.

I watched all the people squirming on the floor as the robber waived his gun at the clerk who dumped the register cash into the black bag.

The robber ran out the door and just left this shocked mass of confused people. Slowly, people started rising and furtively glancing towards the door in case the robber returned. Two men went over to the guy who got slammed into the desk. He groaned as they carefully lifted him out of the pile of glass shards and rolled him onto his stomach. One guy reached for a pair of scissors and gently cut open the back of the man's shirt. It looked like those funeral suits, except this man's back was oozing blood of the injured living.

Finally, everyone sighed in relief as we heard the ambulance and cops approaching.

My mother lost her twenty dollars for the telephone bill, but she did not care because we were both safe.

I slept so strangely that night. It was like I was both deeply asleep from the exhaustion of the day but at the same time completely awake and aware of everything happening around me. It was like my hearing had become like a new extension of my vision. I was so aware of everything.

The next morning, I was assaulted in a different way as I entered my school — noxious fumes of sulphur permeated every air molecule of our school's classrooms and hallways. Angry students sat next to the windows as the smell of rotten eggs seeped into their nostrils. A rumor swirled among the fart stench that this was payback to the History teacher from a disgruntled student.

I did not care that much about the smell because my seat was next to the window and I laughed thinking to myself that everyone was going to fail his tests from now on.

The walk home that day was one of the best of my life — I had the adrenaline kick of loving life after the robbery experience as I inhaled the sweetest, purest air of my life. I chuckled to myself as I entered the house and saw my mom cleaning the kitchen. She looked perfectly fine for someone who had just experienced a robbery, so I decided to relax in my room.

In all the hubbub at school, I had seen a flyer announcing baseball team tryouts in four days. I pulled the flyer out from my bag and checked the date on my calendar.

This reminded me of when I had been in the ROTC, which I had joined because I liked holding the decorative rifles for the unarmed drill team. In the color guard, we learned patterned formations where two riflemen and two flag bearers spun their rifles and flags, respectively. But it became boring and disorganized after the C.O. graduated, so I quit and found myself with too much time on my hands.

This baseball team sounded like a perfect outlet for my energy.

I was so nervous during the tryouts because I did not want to embarrass myself, so I tried my very best. I ran every base full speed and stretched my mitt to catch every ball. I was happy that I got put on the JV team, but then a fire grew in me. I wanted to play first base, but I needed to work hard.

I threw myself into practice and pumped myself up for our first game, which our trembling hands and insecure attitudes made us lose. I was so upset that I just felt quiet. I did not give up hope, though, and persevered even though we continued to lose games.

In my junior year, my coach really connected with me, as I was able to understand more of what his advice meant and how to bring the skills of that advice to the field. Three others and I became alternates for the Varsity team and were asked to go on a trip during spring break to Arizona to play an away game.

I tried to contain my excitement and I played it cool until I got home where I nearly shouted the news to my mom.

On the morning of the trip, she woke me up at 4 am, but I was still awake from the night before. I had not slept a wink and it was torture lifting my exhausted body out of bed. My sloth arms clawed at my shirt as I struggled to get it over my head.

Dawn was breaking over the school as the coach seated us in the two vans that would carry us to Arizona. I pumped myself up reminding my droopy eyelids that someone would mess with me if I fell asleep.

We pulled out of the school parking lot and were on our way. I was in a middle seat and strained to keep my concentration on the passing view of the city of L.A. that was waking up. But exhaustion crept over my body and tugged my eyelids down like the shades of a window.

I slept a dreamless sleep until someone rapped me on my head. It woke me like it was a nightmare itself. I was annoyed and glanced at the angelic faces of the row of teammates sitting behind me.

I decided to stay awake for the rest of the trip.

After five hours, all of our butts were numb as our vans pulled into a dusty desert area where no grass could be seen. Thank heavens we found relief in the pool they had at the motel we were staying.

We found out a lot about each other because of the pool. For example, Tony could not swim. This was only discovered after my friends and I threw his unsuspecting body into the aqua waters where he splashed around like brain-damaged fish. At first we thought he was playing with us, but then we could not deny that he was staying under the water for too long.

We fished him out and left him sputtering on dry land. This incident did not dissuade us from ambushing all of our teammates who all surrendered to their watery fates, except Adrian who fought like a muscular wiggle worm whose life depended on staying above the fray.

The next day, we had to put on our game faces to play three baseball games instead of just two like the other teams. I had a boring day of just watching varsity team play since I was not on the roster. I do not know if I could have helped my team, but we got creamed in the first and second games. But we did nearly win the third game.

On Wednesday, we continued throwing teammates into the pool. After we became bored with this, we decided to have our own baseball tournament and then our own boxing matches. We must have looked a little strange since we only had one set of boxing gloves, which we separated and gave one to each contender. I had my first fight in my entire life against my friend Juan. I loved it and felt so alive after the match.

After that, we went back to playing baseball games against other teams. On that Thursday, we lost a bracket match; but then after that we won our first game!

We celebrated by going to Sonic. It was a big deal for me because I could hear my dad lecturing me in the back of my mind saying, "That restaurant is too expensive. It's a waste of money. You shouldn't eat that. You're too fat already." But today he was back at home and I was a winner celebrating with my friends.

When we got back to the hotel, we were all stuffed and exhausted from the game and the fun. So, our coach let us watch a scary movie. I do not like scary movies because they always give me nightmares. I don't even know what the name of the movie was but I tried to avoid watching the gore and hearing the pleas and screams of the hapless victims. I just focused my eyes and ears on my phone where I was watching the movie *Field of Dreams* for about the hundredth time.

Most of the players were asleep but then the coach started riling everyone up by telling us stories about how he heard that the hotel was haunted and that a whole team of baseball players had been found murdered there in the 1950s. I hated that he was saying these silly things.

I hated it because I knew it was untrue and I hated it because it was getting inside my mind. Some of the guys wanted to go outside and check around the hotel for ghosts. I knew this was stupid, but I went along with them because I knew I would never sleep now.

It was cold outside and I shoved my hands in my pockets. But the fear was starting to build in me as we played a hybrid version of hide-and-seek/tag in the parking lot. Jose was "It" and he lumbered around like a Frankenstein as his shadow played in the misty air. I was crouched behind a red Mustang and had my hand on the slick chrome of the hubcap.

I could see stupid Jose acting like an idiot jumping on unsuspecting players who were hiding in different places. The caught people had to go stand in the center of the parking lot. I had my eyes trained and strained on Jose and the other caught people, but the hairs on the back of my neck were still tingling.

Something's behind me.

Someone's behind me!

"Augh!"

I huge hand gripped my shoulder and a voice boomed, "BOOOO!"

"Coach! Stop it!" I said in anger as I resigned myself to joining the losers huddled in the parking lot center. This was turning into a long night.

Finally Friday pre-dawn turned into Friday itself as we all headed out to a ceremony related to the founding of the tournament. The local players all stood in formation and saluted the statue of an American soldier who had played baseball but had died in combat.

I feel guilty to admit that the ceremony speaker was a monotonous bore who droned on and on. I felt bad that this soldier had died and this speaker was the vehicle for him to be remembered because no one would remember anything of the tedious speech.

My mind drifted to thoughts about how the soldier had lived and died. Had he gotten his comrades to play baseball when they were on leave from fighting? Did the people he fought against like to play baseball, too? What other countries is baseball popular in?

Our time in Arizona ended and we made it back to California around 9 pm.

The very next day, Jesus and Anita invited me to the Magic Johnson Park to hang out. I was surprised that they wanted to hang out outside of school, but I was game. We met halfway from my place to the park then we all took turns walking and riding Jesus' bike.

At the park, Jesus peddled around the duck pond and Anita and I watched a father and his two kids feed bread to the ducks, which gobbled up every morsel. Every time the younger kid threw bread to the ducks, the little piece landed on one duck's head. The duck would shake his head in annoyance and make this little duck "roar" sound. We all laughed every time.

Jesus rejoined us and we all walked over to the bridge and sat on the railing to look at the ducks that were ducking their heads under water and preening themselves. We started to compare ourselves to the different ducks. The big duck was I; the small one was Jesus; and, the smallest duck hanging out with the other two ducks was Anita. Slowly, the big and little duck moved away from the smallest one and she started to look sad and cold.

We all felt a little strange and I wanted to break up this sudden gloom.

"Hey, let's go get some food at the Burger King," I said with forced joy.

It was a good decision because getting away from the ducks lightened our mood. I got just a regular hamburger (I thought my dad would commend me for foregoing the cheese) and Anita and Jesus both got cheeseburgers. We walked back to the park, but the gloom returned as we stumbled on a dead, rotting squirrel. It must have fallen from the tree and then other animals had ravaged its intestines. The squirrel's face was frozen in a scrawling scream.

Anita was visibly upset and just threw her burger in the trash without even unwrapping it. Jesus and I were still hungry and we sat on some rocks as we scarfed down our meal. Anita sat on her own rock as she looked over the water. She seemed distracted and upset.

"You know my ex-boyfriend?" she ventured.

Jesus and I both looked up with quizzical expressions on our faces. She rarely brought him up. We had no idea that things were about to get crazy.

"I saw him with another girl," Anita said sadly.

Jesus said that he knew.

Anita's face flared with anger, "What do you mean that you know?"

Oh, Jesus, you f*cked up.

Jesus looked like he knew he had f*cked up, but he tried to play it off by saying, "Oh, don't worry about it. I thought you didn't care about him anymore."

"I don't care. But…maybe I do care," Anita said in confusion. "Why didn't you tell me, anyway?"

"I don't know. I didn't think about it. You said you didn't care," Jesus rejoined.

This started into a mind-numbing volley of the same toxic things being said back and forth, back and forth. They were trapped in some verbal loop and I was angrily standing on the outside unable to penetrate their hurtful retorts to each other.

It was just like my parents and the cancerous anger welled up in me as my frustration fumed.

This kind of thing was why I could not feel any deep emotions anymore. I could only make jokes and talk about superficial things. I could not afford to delve into emotions or delve into relationships.

What if Anita and Jesus stopped being friends with each other and I had to choose between them?

Then it really would have mimicked my relationship with my parents.

How had this afternoon taken such a turn for the worse?

Then, I realized that Jesus had started talking about how he thought he was a negative part of his family and that he was causing his family so many problems. He was crying and Anita was crying and holding him.

I clenched my jaw tight and strengthened myself against starting to cry.

I will not cry.

I cannot cry.

"Hey, you guys," I tried to feign a lighthearted tone. "It's a great day and we're all together. Let's enjoy the afternoon! Let's leave all this behind us."

Jesus and Anita dried their tears and fell silent as they held each other and looked out over the water. We saw the three ducks from before huddled in a corner of the pond.

We started to walk home as Jesus slowly pedaled his bike and Anita and I walked alongside.

Anita seemed lost in thought and then suddenly she turned to me and asked, "Why didn't you care when Jesus was talking about his family?"

My eyes darted to Jesus but he just acted like he did not hear us and pedaled ahead.

"I don't know. I guess I'm just not a crier," I lamely said.

"I don't think you needed to cry. But it was like you didn't care at all," she said.

"I'm just not emotional," I continued.

"You're a stone statue. I hate that about you," she fired back.

She had cut me to the core and I retorted, "Well, maybe I am. Maybe I can't feel anything."

I walked ahead of her towards Jesus, who circled his bike back around to rejoin us.

When we got to my house, I said my good-byes to them as they slowly made their way back to the street and headed back to their own homes.

Safely in my room, my mind pondered the events of the afternoon. Thoughts darted around my mind.

I do not know how I am going to survive this life where I am afraid to feel things or make relationships. I just do not want to get caught in caring for people or get caught choosing between people. It is a painful life, but it is less painful than the alternative.

Later that day, I went to my dad's house and then I went over to Bryan and Bobby's place to hang out. We usually played video games but sometimes we went out and roasted on each other. At first, I did not use to hang out with Bryan and Bobby too often, but then we hung out more often. I learned a lot from Bobby, who was pretty much the brother I always wanted. He told me great tips about how to survive in this life. I thought that if I stuck with him, he could make me a lot smarter because he had a huge bank of knowledge.

Bobby had a sister named Blanca who was a cool girl but we always acted like we hated one another. I liked to provoke her by asking the family who they would rather have live at their house — Blanca or me.

And, they always chose me.

When I got home, my dad said that he wanted to go out to eat.

"Can't we eat something here?" I asked.

"No, I don't want to bring food in the house because either your uncles will just eat or the cockroaches will eat it," my father resolutely said as he pushed his arm through the sleeve of his jacket.

At the IHop, I slid into the booth and wished we had sat at a regular table. My chubby stomach touched the table, but I could not move the table or my dad would notice and lecture me about being too fat. This whole situation was a minefield. I scanned the menu for anything that I could order that would not lead my dad to lecturing me.

Pancakes? Nope.

Pasta? Nope.

If I ordered the salad, then he would say that it was not enough food and I would quickly be hungry later.

What could I do?

This was like everything else.

If I were on my phone with friends, he would nag me that I should be reading a book. If I wanted a new book to read, he would complain that it was too expensive to always buy books that I just read once and put on a shelf. If I asked him to drive me to library, he would say that everything I wanted to do takes too much time. I was too fat, anyway, and I should walk there myself.

It was really an unpleasant maze with no reward of cheese.

Everything was nonsensical and difficult with my dad. I came to realize that he could restart an argument from a week ago. He could talk trash about my mom about something she supposedly did years ago. I learned to just silently endure these tirades. Whenever I walked down the path from my mom's house to his car, I tried to read his face to gauge what type of mood he was in. It was exhausting.

The only thing that I ever did that made my father happy was playing baseball. Ironically, this thing was a nail in my mother's coffin. One day, we had a car wash to raise money for my baseball team. Of course, my mom joined in. We do not know exactly what happened, but we heard a scream and found my mom had slipped down three flights of stairs.

Her leg was broken and she suffers to this day. She cannot work and depends on my uncle to pay her thirty dollars each time he eats with us. It is a strange arrangement because he eats food with us and then gives us money that my mother uses to buy food for the family. I do not know if I understand the logic of it.

But as I continue with life, I realize that we cannot complain about what happens to us or to our loved ones.

Epilogue

Someone is waking me from a dream. I open my eyes and remember that I slept over at Bryan's house on his sofa.

"Hey, man," Bryan says. "Do you want to go to the park?"

"Yeah," I say, as I rub my eyes.

As we enter the park, Bryan sees some friends and goes over to chat with them. I settle on a bench and watch some young kids playing baseball. One kid slides into home base on a wing and a prayer. He must have skinned the outside of this leg because he gets up hopping on one leg and immediately starts to cry. The kid who is playing catcher for the other team goes over to help him. The hurt kid sucks it up and stops crying.

Later I see him up at bat again and do another fearless dash for a base. I feel like he is showing me a perfect metaphor for my own American story.

Life is like a sport. You know that you are going to get hurt. So, all you can do is get back up and continue with the game of life.

12

Against all Odds

By

Gilberto J Avalos

Chapter 1

"Five Days until this Summer 2016 El Paso High School Graduation," Principal Miller said on the old scratchy intercom.

I remember that day everyone was jumping around screaming with joy, but I wasn't. I needed a cold wind to cool me. I felt like I was about to have a stroke.

Graduation day was upon us.

"Antonio Hernandez for valedictorian," announced Principal Miller.

I sat on the podium in my assigned seat as I peered over the crowd that became a single photograph of an image waving in the dire heat.

The principal droned on, "Antonio has been a model student who has dedicated himself to every project and has been an inspiration in his efforts to graduate at the top of his class."

As he mumbled on, a sense of pride started to grow inside me during this strange moment where I felt so introspective while I was actually sitting in front of a large audience.

"And, now, ladies and gentlemen, please give a round of applause for your valedictorian," the principal called out like a game show host.

As I stood and adjusted my black robe that was sticking to my sweating body, I began to walk across the dais. But with each step the deafening silence of the proud mothers and fathers of all my classmates stirred the pain and envy that was killing me inside.

I broke down crying, grabbed by diploma, and stormed off the dais.

Chapter 2

I escaped to my sanctuary under the bleachers at a nearby park where I watched the day grow shorter as night began to walk the tightrope of twisted memories in my mind. The tightrope held the story my grandmother had told me when I was fourteen about my parent's death.

"They were killed in an accident when they were on the way to pick you up from my house," she said the first time and every time after that.

It was so little information that I guess I began to imagine details and add them to the events of that day. They were driving a red car and were hit by a blue truck. No, they were driving a blue car and were hit by a silver truck. They were singing along with the radio that was playing their favorite song. No, they were talking about how they hoped I would go to university one day.

In truth, I had been getting angrier all graduation day morning as I saw students brushing away their moms who tried to straighten their children's caps. I felt exasperated as I overheard students arguing with their parents about borrowing the family car to go to a party that night instead of going to the dinner that was planned with their grandparents.

Those kids did not even know how lucky they were!

This perspective had fueled me on for all my years of high school. As I studied deep into the night, I would imagine that very graduation moment where an undocumented kid with no parents would have topped everyone in school and in life. I will not lie — I feared that I would be eclipsed by someone who was smarter or more diligent than I was. But so far, I had beaten the odds of this messed up utopia where minorities are pushed to gutters.

Emotions filled my mouth with bitterness as I spurned myself on towards the giant flashing sign above Jackie's Liquors. It burned my swollen eyes and I hoped the alcohol would burn my throat and burn out my memories.

Through the door's glass, I could see the drunk Tony passed out on the store floor still holding his cheap gasoline-like vodka in his lap. I gingerly opened the door that still jingled the small bell attached to the top.

Al, a giant man with red hair and a beer belly, looked up from studying the lottery tickets that people threw away in the trash. He always bragged about that one time someone threw away a hundred-dollar winning ticket. He was rumored to be a former lumberjack who had come down from Seattle after some environmentalists had shut down his lumber mill. Whatever had happened, he had a past and he carried an anger that I never wanted to see in action.

"Just getting a coke, Al," I cheerfully said in a low voice as I blanked the Jack Daniels on sale on the display near the front.

It took nearly all of my strength to muster that false joy. All I needed to do was create a distraction to get Al's suspicious eyes off my back. I had a quick flash of Al sliding a massive log into a glinting, maniacal saw blade.

Dirty Tony's slumbering grunt brought me back to the task at hand. I walked to the back case filled with beer. I walked over to the case of sodas that was closest to the beers in their breakable glass bottles. The soda case offered about seven different variations of Coke — yeah, the land of plenty. I glanced up to the mirror in the back wall's upper corner to check on Al's location — yeah, two could play at this game.

Crash, pop, crash, fizz, crash!

"What the hell!" Al shouted as he made his way to the back as I made my way to the front holding the Diet Coke Zero in front of me like a safety pass.

"Sorry, man, I don't know what happened. I just reached in for the…" I stammered.

"Get outta my way," the old grizzly snorted as pushed passed me to investigate the beer case.

I tried to keep my pace casual, but I hurried up to the front display, grabbed that liter of Jack Daniels, and ran out into the pitch blackness.

My ears burned with the shouts of that lumberjack threatening to call the cops as I sprinted into night.

Chapter 3

No longer a valedictorian, I became a criminal.

Was I a man or a machine?

I felt my heart pumping fuel throughout my being like a drag racer who has fused with his vehicle. It was one of the best feelings I had ever felt.

Adrenaline carried my being to the water tower where I climbed up it to sit on the edge. I promptly opened the pilfered bottle and took swig after swig. Lost in thought, I waited for the dawn and began to make my way home.

My grandmother smothered me in her embrace and she sobbed, "I thought you were dead. Some boy got shot in the street last night."

She was hysterical and had been crying all night. She had a headache; she felt dizzy. She could not speak. She clutched my arms and then wilted as I staggered to keep her from falling.

At first I thought she had just fainted. I lowered her to the floor and grabbed a dishtowel to put under her head.

"Abuela, abuela," I called into her unconscious face.

I knew instantly that this was not just a fainting spell, but a stroke.

Regret and guilt burrowed into my stomach as the paramedics lifted her limp form into the back of the ambulance. I had caused this stroke by running away from my problems and drowning my sorrows in a bottle of liquor. As I tightly held her lifeless hand on the drive to the hospital, I wondered to myself how yesterday morning before the graduation ceremony had turned into this morning with my life in pieces.

The next morning, the doctors said that she was stabilized, so I returned home to shower. As I walked out the door to go pick up her medicine, I got the mail from our box.

"Urgent," screamed the big red letters on the envelope from the Powell and Mitchell Immigration Law Firm.

I took a deep breath and sliced open the envelope to read the enclosed letter. Finally, a piece of good news. The fee I had paid for the pardon of entering the country illegally had been fully processed and I was about to become a naturalized citizen. Of course, there was catch. I was required to spend the next two weeks in my home state of Tijuana, Mexico in order to officially return as a newly minted U.S. citizen.

You cannot become a U.S. citizen if you stay here; you cannot stay here if you are not a U.S. citizen.

A perfect Catch-22.

What was not perfect was that the doctors dropped a bomb that afternoon — tests had shown that my grandmother had early signs of stomach cancer.

Chapter 4

After my grandmother was discharged from the hospital, we returned home and settled into a strange sense of suspended reality. School was finished and I was absorbed with caring for my grandmother who had been given a set of daily exercises to strengthen her grip and to strengthen her memory and speech skills.

Whenever I blinked, let alone closed my eyes to try to sleep, the bold, red letters on the lawyer's envelope flashed in my mind: URGENT.

I wanted to stay and care for my grandmother, but I knew that she would encourage me to go as this would be a huge step in my ability to get scholarships for university.

"Please, don't go. Don't go. Don't leave me here," she begged.

I was surprised, but I tried to hide it. Maybe her pain was worse than I realized.

Maybe she was afraid of dying alone. Maybe she was just afraid of dying.

I had not expected this turmoil. I had expected to fight against her wishes for me to go; instead, I found myself fighting against her wishes for me to stay.

But guilt still racked my being.

Should I stay and nurse the only person who had given me food, shelter, and clothing?

Or, should I go and pursue my path to my long-term future?

"Grandma?" I whispered as she lay on her bed.

"Yes," she feebly answered. "I know you have to go."

The relief washed over me as my shoulders shook as I struggled to hold back the tears.

"I'm sorry for hurting you," I managed to say.

Her pride returned as she stiffened and said, "What makes you think that? I can handle myself. You know, I have fought all my life for your mother and for you. This is a moment not just for you, but for all of us."

I held her hand even tighten than when we had ridden in the ambulance and said, "Aprovecha el momento, no lo malgastes."

All was understood and she released my hand and reached for the television remote control as I turned to my room to pack for my trip to TJ.

I grabbed my old leather travel bag from atop the bookcase filled with knowledge from every subject.

Would this book learning help me navigate the seedy world of TJ? And, if I survived TJ, would I be able to navigate the next steps in the bureaucracy of naturalization?

The TV blared in the background, "The leader of the notorious La Muerta Blanca was assassinated last year in a shootout with a rival cartel while the scattered remnants of this violent group were taken out in police sting operations. But this resilient force has been reborn."

I half-listened as I folded shirts and pants, but I could see my grandmother's body was stiff with attention. She always hated this gang in particular.

"Although the leader's son Santiago de Blanca has mainly been seen at his villa in Italy, in the past few months he has been increasingly spotted in the border town of Tijuana," the journalist continued.

My ears perked up at the mention of TJ as I rolled pairs of socks.

Why did she always follow news about de Blanca?

"International monitors have reported a sharp increase in drugs being moved across the border from Mexico into the United States as well as a marked increase in gang related violence and retaliatory killings," the journalists reported.

I shoved this information out of my mind and closed the lid on my suitcase. My grandmother snorted in anger as they began to list the suspected murders associated with cartel.

Chapter 5

After I finished packing my bags, I returned to the living room to find my grandmother asleep with the news continuing about car crashes and other terrible things happening in the world. I did not want her sleeping with those things creeping into her mind. I turned off the television.

She must have felt me looking at her and her eyes fluttered awake and blinked in the early shafts of morning light.

"No, no, Grandma. Sleep longer," I said. "I'll wake you before I go."

She was having none of that and pushed herself out of the chair and went directly to my room where she fished around in my suitcase to make sure I had packed everything I would need.

"Grandma, I'm not a child," I said in frustration, but actually it made me feel special that she still cared so much for me after all I had put her through in the past weeks.

I left her to add small things to my bag and went to take in the mail. As I went outside into the periwinkle world of calm, an ominous wind blew around and whispered indistinguishable words in my ear. My subconscious leaned in to hear the words that faded away.

When I returned to the kitchen, my grandmother was sitting at the small table with her face in her hands.

She looked up at me and said, "I lied to you."

I knew in my gut, in my spirit that she was talking about the death of my parents.

"What really happened?" I asked.

"It wasn't an accident," she gravely said.

Her brow furrowed and I could feel her throat tightening with anxiety, desperation, and fear.

My brow furrowed in frustration and my throat loosened with all the anger that I wanted to express. Every one of her words became one of the rocks thrown from the Bible's David at Goliath. David was the hard truth and Goliath had been the warm bubble of deceitful protection that she had wrapped around me.

"Just tell me everything. Who knows what is going to happen in the next few weeks. I deserve to know. I am a man now," I stated point blank.

"You can't go to TJ," she sputtered.

This again!

"What happened to my parents?" I asked as I tried to steer the conversation back to something tangible. Obviously, there was something deeper going on about my parent's death and my going to TJ.

"They started off wanting to fight against the corrupt government, the police, and the cartels. But they became jaded and, eventually, became what they hated most. They became targets for La

Muerta Blanca who viewed them as rivals," she said with great
sadness.

I inhaled deeply — my life of a few weeks ago was like the life
of a different person. But in times of great stress, there can be great
clarity. It was live or die.

And I was making a choice — I would either have a real life of a
naturalized American citizen or I would become just another dead
Mexican kid in Tijuana.

"Grandma, I'm going to Tijuana and I'm going to survive and
return to the U.S. I'm leaving in fifteen minutes with or without your
blessing," I said with a renewed sense of following through on all the
dreams I had worked for during the last four years of my life.
Somehow, that moment became my graduation speech.

My grandma sighed and reached for the small container of sugar
that had set on our kitchen table for as long as I could remember. She
lifted it and suddenly unscrewed the circular bottom to reveal a
hiding spot. It contained several pieces of thin paper about the size of

a business card. She withdrew one of the pieces of paper and pressed the yellowed slip of paper into my palm.

"This is the name and address of your aunt in Tijuana. She will protect you," my Grandma answered.

RING! RING!

The telephone startled us out of that moment of family secrets.

While my grandma stood to answer the phone, I sat in shock as I read through the old-fashioned handwriting on the paper. But my attention was quickly drawn to the voice on the other end of the phone call whose message I could hear loud and clear.

"Hello. This is the El Paso Police Department and we're calling about the whereabouts of Mr. Antonio J. Hernandez. He's wanted for robbery at Jackie's Liquors. If you have any information regarding this, please call (915)-030-3150," the voice blankly stated.

All the blood ran to my face and I looked down in shame and self-castigation.

My grandmother just shook her head.

"You are a wanted man — if you go to TJ, you'll be charged with fleeing the country," she said.

"But if I don't go, I can't become a citizen," I responded helplessly.

"What? You're going to become a proud citizen of a country where you live in a jail for stealing from a liquor store?" she asked with frustration.

"Grandma, what can I do?" I asked in a lost tone.

I knew she loved me and was just beyond knowing what to do.

"You have only one real choice — go to TJ tonight and stay with your aunt. Don't talk to anyone. Don't tell anyone anything. If anyone who doesn't have the right to see your papers asks, tell them your name is Juan Garcia. Only answer yes or no to any question," she answered in a fiery tone I had never heard before.

"Juan Garcia?" I meekly asked.

She stomped to the bedroom and grabbed my suitcase.

She pressed the bag into my hands and said, "It's the most common name in Mexico. Where is the paper with your aunt's information?"

"It's here safely in my pocket," I answered as I reached into the front of my jeans to withdraw the paper just as I felt a hand slap my left cheek.

My grandmother had never hit me before.

"Safely in your pocket? That little piece of paper would be your death sentence. Get your wits together! Memorize it!" she said with eyes blazing and she snatched the paper and replaced it in the sugar bowl bottom.

I hugged her angry form and left to try to survive this two-week purgatory.

Chapter 6

Was I the good guy or the bad guy?

I grabbed my things and walked out the door to leave when the crackle of a megaphone coming to life startled me.

"Antonio J. Hernandez, this is the El Paso Police Department. We know you're in there. Come out with your hands up! We've got you surrounded," the monotone voice boomed.

Why was this happening all over a stolen bottle of liquor? This was overkill!

I had fought against all the odds so hard for so long that a deep matrix of resolve burned to life in my gut. I would not just go down without a fight. I had fought my whole life to be a top student and to become a naturalized citizen who could have the future he wanted and did not have to look over his shoulder for guerrillas, gang members, or immigration police.

I tightened my backpack to my back as I saw my grandmother huddled under the kitchen table. I thought about how the generations of my family had supported me to get me to the point where I even had a future to fight for. I thought about the name that was on that piece of paper and I jumped out the window.

In the roving floodlights, I could see glimmers of glass shards sticking out of my bleeding arms that looked like someone had spilled communion wine all down my arm and leg. I would have to deal with that later.

I ran and ran and I felt another type of kinship — that of with Elie Wiesel. He had run in the Nazi camp — his lungs burning as he was chased. He had wanted to give up, but he did not. He had burned on and he had survived.

I made it to the bus station and kept my eyes on the ground as I quickly went into the men's bathroom. I went into the handicapped stall and looked over my arm. I winced as I pulled the larger shards of glass out of my arm. I heard other people flushing the toilets and washing their hands. I waited till the bathroom was empty and quickly went out to the sink and ran my arm under the cold water.

The water was like a cold fire that burned and soothed my arm.

I wadded up my ruined hoodie to cover the bloodstains and dumped it in the trash. I quickly slid back into the handicapped stall to get out a new hoodie. I wrapped my arm in a black T-shirt and I could feel the remaining glass slivers digging deeper into my skin. I winced and pulled the fresh hoodie over my head.

I bought a ticket to cross the border. I inhaled with the thought that if this trip went well, I could safely and legally cross back over this border — this fictitious, man-made division between nations, between peoples, between opportunities.

As I took the bus ticket in my fingers I could see that my hands were shaking from adrenaline, fear, and excitement.

Chapter 7

I slept the whole bus ride and was awakened by the bus driver shaking my injured arm. The glass slivers pierced my nerves and I yelped in pain.

The bus driver recoiled in surprise.

"Sorry, I was having a nightmare," I lamely explained.

The bus station depot was filled with aggressive taxi drivers who fought with each other as they competed to underbid one another for customers. Exhausted, I ignored the fray and walked straight to an older taxi driver who was reading a newspaper.

"Can you take me to La Calle — ?" I asked.

He eyed me up and down and said a reasonable price.

I jumped in the back and we started out in the streets of Tijuana, a hubbub of every kind of activity from drunken white kids from L.A. getting cheap prescription meds to the roving sets of black SUVs that monitored their cartel's territory. The taxi driver scowled at the idiotic drunks throwing their lives away but paled at the SUVs that ferried around drug lords and fearsome henchmen.

My thoughts returned to my Aunt, whose name was Rebecca. I did not know what to expect of her and I suspected that she was somehow involved in the world of the cartels, like my parents had been.

As the taxi slowly made it its way towards the stated address, I noticed a mansion on top of a hill. The surrounding neighborhoods were all crummy slums that reminded me of the Buenos Aires favelas. I saw dogs eating scraps from the garbage next to children in dirty clothes eating similar scraps. I wanted to wretch, not from disgust for what these children were doing to survive, but wretch out of disgust for what humanity allowed to happen.

As the taxi kept winding up the hill closer and closer to the mansion, I finally asked and got confirmation that we were going to the mansion on the hill. The lights shone brightly like eyes staring at me. It was like a well-lit version of the house from the movie *Psycho*.

"Estás aqui," the taxi driver said.

I paid him and turned to the mansion's gate to look for an intercom.

Did my Aunt Rebecca know that I was coming?

A loud buzz of the gate startled me as the lights over the gate flashed on and the side door for pedestrians swung open. From the side door, I could see the silhouette of a woman.

It was my aunt.

She welcomed me with open arms. And, as I smelled her hair and skin, a primal memory of my mother's embrace flooded my psyche. My connection to my aunt was immediate.

"Come in, come in, dear," she said as she ushered me on to the mansion grounds.

She held me around my waist as we walked towards the mansion whose window-eyes seemed to be sizing me up as allowed entry or not.

"When you parents died, they left me all their money," Rebecca explained as she pushed open the massive front door.

As I settled into Rebecca's house, I thought about how my grandma had taken me across the border so I would not be killed by the cartel and so I would have opportunities to live a healthy and happy life. Because I felt so appreciative for everything she had done, I decided to use some of the money I still had to buy my grandma a ticket to meet us in Tijuana.

After I bought the ticket, I called her to tell her.

"I'll be there in two days," she said excitedly over the phone. "I can't believe our family will be together again."

Was my whole family going to be rejoined in Tijuana?

I felt like I was in this strange limbo world where I was not sure if I should feel like I was a part of Rebecca's Tijuana world or still a part of my grandma's Los Angeles world. But I guess things were being decided for me.

I called my Los Angeles lawyer to see how my case was going. After all, I had only stolen a bottle of liquor. Maybe it would just be a fine?

"They want to send you to jail for three to six months," the lawyer said matter-of-factly.

"That's crazy! How can they justify that? It's my first offense," I said while I gripped the phone.

I was shattered and I slammed the phone down. I guess my life was going to be in Tijuana. Luckily, when I asked Rebecca about finding any local work, she had just the job for me.

"Yes, you can be a courier for our family business," she smiled with assurance.

"What does that mean I'll be doing?" I asked.

"You'll be taking packages from place to place — just like FedEx," she answered.

"And, I'll get paid for this?" I asked.

"Of course," she laughed. "But we work with different powerful businesses that must keep their proposals private. So, you must never look in the packages under any circumstances," she added in a serious tone.

With this, she reached into her wallet and handed me a fat wad of cash that she called an advance on my future earnings.

"Now, your Grandma will be arriving any minute from the bus station," she said as she looked at her watch.

That evening, I was thrilled that things were looking better. My Grandma was with me, I had a new aunt, and I had a high-paying job. My grandma's eyes happily glowed with a burning flame that showed her former energy had been restored.

That week, I began my courier job in earnest. I delivered package after package to address after address. I was exhausted, but I was learning to navigate the city and I was pleased with my payouts.

It was late on a typical evening and I had one more package to deliver. I drove my car towards the drop off place, when, suddenly, shots rang out!

As I peeled out of there, I looked in the rear view mirror and saw two guys peeling out in the opposite direction. I shifted the gears and thrust the car into overdrive to return to my aunt's house. But when I was stopped at a traffic light, I noticed a strange white powder spilling out of the package on the passenger seat.

Everything made sense now — the secrecy about the packages, random locations, tension, and large amounts of money — I had been delivering cocaine.

When I pulled up to the house, I could sense that everything was wrong.

Sure enough, I found my grandmother crying on the sofa. When she turned her head to see me, I could tell that she had a black eye and bruises all over her.

"Rebecca?" I called out for help and I rushed to my grandma's side.

"They took your aunt!" my grandma said and she held onto me.

I was enraged, but I knew what needed to be done.

"Who took her?" I said trying to be calm.

"Santiago de Blanca," she yelled out like a screaming banshee.

Chapter 8

I jumped back in my car and took a deep breath as I turned the key in the ignition. Fate had brought me to this moment and what was destined to happen was about to happen. I strengthened my resolve and drove out of the driveway to find my aunt.

Only one place stuck out in my mind as a possible place where they might hold her. My aunt had told me about an old abandoned ranch where she and my mom used to hide out from cops and rivals. Now, it was going to be the place where I would die.

I sped to the old ranch, but then slowed to a quiet crawl as I spied the main gate. I stealthily parked behind a large set of trees and then covertly made my way up to the ranch. I saw a trail of blood in the dust and footprints leading up to the house.

I wondered if they would accept a trade of me for Rebecca.

As I neared the porch, the unmistakable wretched odor of dead corpses and dried blood filled the air. It was poison to my lungs and I stifled my coughs of disgust. There were no sounds from within and I peered through the windows to find an empty house. I carefully

opened the door and silently entered the dangerously still house. I

could barely see in the dark house but finally found a staircase and

started upstairs.

Cobwebs slowed my ascent until I finally reached the top

hallway. I could hear muffled voices inside a room. I made my way

to the door and tried to sneak a look through the crack in the door and

saw my aunt tied to a chair — SHOTS! SCREAMS!

A bodyguard roughly grabbed me and pulled me in the room.

"So, boy, you've come to be killed along with your pathetic

aunt?" the leader asked.

I struggled to make my voice confident as I answered, "I'm here

for my aunt."

I looked into her dark eyes as she looked back at me with

intensity.

"Brave you are — you sure are a brave one," he said in a tone

that mimicked a tongue twister.

"What are you inferring — that I'm afraid of you? You've kidnapped a woman. Why don't you take me instead?" I said as I tried to mediate the anger in my voice.

Our conversation was cut short as a hail of bullets shattered the windows.

The cartel bodyguards immediately returned gunfire as I dove behind my aunt. I worked to untie her hands and we both ran in a crouched position to the hallway. The bodyguards were being dropped one-by-one as my aunt and I huddled under a downstairs window.

"Come out with your hands up!" I heard the familiar sound of police surrounding the house.

I waved my hand in the window in a sign of peace.

"Don't shoot. I'm just a kid!" I shouted to them.

"Show yourself!" the voice boomed through the megaphone.

I slowly stood in the window and shouted back, "My aunt is here, too."

"Both of you come out with your hands up!" the voice instructed.

My aunt and I slowly made our way to the front door and carefully exited the house.

At first, I felt relief that my aunt and I had survived the gunfight, but I was quickly filled with horror as I saw my grandmother's body lying on the ground next to one of the police cars. She had been shot during the gun battle.

I did not care what the officers were shouting — I raced to my grandmother's side. I held her dying body in my arms.

"What are you doing here?" I asked as tears filled my eyes.

"I called the police and told them what had happened. We all came here to save you," she explained.

"Why is everything so terrible?" I asked in frustration.

"No, it's not. You will survive this and you will live your dreams. I love you — promise me you'll be safe and live an honest life," she whispered with her dying breath.

I realized that my aunt had used me as a pawn in her drug running business and that I wanted nothing to do with her anymore. I did truly want to live an honest life and pursue my dreams.

My grandmother's light fell into darkness and her inner flame was extinguished. Those were her last words and I broke into tears at my aunt's betrayal and at my grandma's death.

I stood up as a new man and said in my heart:

For you Grandma, I promise you that I will be a success because you helped me against all odds. You did everything and I only hope that I can do the same for others.

Epilogue

For my loved ones, friends, family, Mr. Cubias, Mr. Miller, to everyone who has supported me. And, for the people who don't believe in what people are capable of doing, this is my way of proving them wrong and that people can get done what is right.

Gilberto J. Avalos

13

Unfortunate Flight

By

Saddam Godinez

I walked out of the air-conditioned LAX airport into the dry Los Angeles heat. As I hitched my backpack higher up, I surveyed the crowd for my brother, who was supposed to pick me up. He had had to rearrange his schedule after he got word that I was being sent home on leave from my Iraq deployment.

Cars and taxis jostled with each other to pick up disgruntled relatives, long-time friends, business associates, wanna-be starlets, and general passengers. I scanned the cars for a short guy whose acne could even be seen from a distance.

A dark green Mustang pulled up in front of me and some guy seemed to be waving me out of the way.

Relax, buddy.

But suddenly, the guy stepped half out of his sleek machine and called my name, "Max!"

My brother Johnny had changed a lot since I had been gone.

I awkwardly waved and walked over to the Mustang. My brother slid back into his seat as the traffic captain approached our illegally stopped car. But when he saw my fatigues, the captain nodded and went on his way. I took a moment and slung my knapsack into the backseat.

Was what I did in Iraq worth a few extra minutes of loading time in the airport pick-up lane? Was that the actual payment for what I had done?

"Damn, the weather is way better than it was back there in Iraq," I said with a cringe — not only did I hate chitchat about the weather, I also immediately regretted mentioning Iraq. I slid into the passenger seat and fastened my seatbelt as my brother gave me an awkward hug across the gear shirt.

"Hey, bro," he said. "Glad you're back in one piece," Johnny added as he revved the 300-horsepower machine into action.

While speeding down the highway away from LAX, I watched the planes gracefully maneuver from air to ground. What marvels of modern technology!

We stopped at a red light and I pulled my thoughts back to the tasks at hand.

"Hey, how's Crystal?" I asked my brother about my girlfriend of the past two years.

"She's cool," he said. "But she got really depressed after you left," he added as he swerved to get the off ramp.

When we pulled up to Crystal's house, she was waiting teary-eyed outside the front door. I had sworn I would not cry and I just held her tight and buried my face in her neck. No one would see me break down.

God, she was more beautiful than I remembered.

I inhaled her sweet scent and focused on the happy thought of the trip we planned to take together. I had survived Iraq and we were going to go on our dream vacation to Dubai. But first I needed to visit my mom in Paris and then I was all Crystal's.

Crystal and I settled in that night and she made my favorite dinner. We ate as we surfed the Internet for travel itineraries through Dubai. Without even talking about it, we had avoided making too many plans before I left for my deployment, just in case. We did not need to talk about stuff like that — we had a communion. That was one of the things that I loved about Crystal.

The next morning, I went for a 6 A.M. run through Griffith Park where the cold breeze chilled my face and the smell of the wet dirt was a welcome reminder of my memories before Iraq. At a high ridge, I paused to look over the entirety of downtown Los Angeles, including the pristine white observatory. I imagined being inside the observatory staring up at those magnificent stars that were all staring back at me. Whatever people say about Iraq, you cannot beat the view of the stars at night in that dark desert world.

Back at the house, I showered and made the final reservation for my flight and hotel for my Paris trip to visit with my mother who was a top businesswoman in the fashion industry.

In less than twenty-four hours, I was back at the LAX airport. But this time, Crystal was dropping me off for my ten-and-a-half-hour flight to France.

Even though I had thought we had left with plenty of time to spare, I looked at the airport clock and realized that I was about to miss my flight.

"Last call for flight "113," the loudspeaker announced.

What? How am I late? Did I read the time wrong?

Thoughts darted through my mind as I darted through the maze of lumbering travelers.

Made it!

Sweaty and discombobulated, I plopped into my window seat. The stewardess closed the airplane door latch and the plane began to taxi to the runway. Everything was happening so fast and zoomed straight into lift off.

What a morning!

I scanned the flat valley of Los Angeles with its neighborhoods of two- and three-story buildings built according to earthquake codes and the slice of skyscrapers all huddled together in geological safety zone. The buildings and people receded into miniatures as the plane climbed higher and higher.

When the cars and people both looked like ants, the captain turned off the seat-belt sign and the stewards began serving refreshments. I was exhausted and fell into a deep sleep. I woke rejuvenated and famished. I enjoyed a turkey sandwich and some white wine, which they served in annoying, tiny plastic glasses. I munched my stale sandwich as I killed time by watching *Jurassic Park*, *The Walking Dead*, and *Deadpool*.

The flight was smooth and we touched down in Paris ahead of schedule. Once again, I found myself at an airport pick-up spot craning my neck to find the person who was supposed to get me. It was all the same jostling of people, but with a lot more French thrown in.

Suddenly, a town car pulled up in front of me and I stepped to the side and looked behind me for whichever businessperson who was about to grab his or her ride.

The driver stepped out of the car, looked at me, and asked, "Max?"

"Yes," I quizzically answered as I saw the backseat car window coming down to reveal my mom Amanda's face.

"Hi, sweetie. This is Michel. Let him help you put your bags in the truck," she called out to me.

Well, I guess my mom's business really had taken off.

Michel expertly positioned my bags in the back and whisked us away from the hubbub of the De Gaulle airport.

Inside the luxurious town car, my mom hugged me as Michel smoothly pulled away from the airport fracas.

Paris was even more beautiful than I had imagined. I thought that the Eiffel Tower would look gaudy, but I was taken aback by just how perfectly the architecture created such a balanced structure. I quickly came to realize that my mother had settled into Parisian life, become competent in the language, and developed a vast network of friends and business associates.

The two days passed in a whirlwind and I found myself saying goodbye to my mother at the airport and looking forward to seeing Crystal and visiting Dubai.

Instead of rushing to catch my flight, this time I had plenty of time because my flight was delayed due to thunderstorms in the area. As night descended, I wandered around the overpriced shops and picked out a small snow globe keychain for Crystal.

As I paid, I heard my flight being called and rushed to the gate before I remembered that my mother had bumped me up to first class. I had all the time in the world to leisurely board the plane. My seat was plush and roomy and could be converted into a bed. This was going to be fantastic! As the plane ascended, I took one last look at the city of lights and quickly fell asleep.

I was dreaming of Crystal and me returning to Paris for our honeymoon when I was suddenly awakened by turbulence as someone gasped and I saw her glass of wine tumble into the aisle. I blinked around and looked outside the dark windows and could see thick, angry clouds illuminated by the wing's lights.

The cabin lights surged into power and the seatbelt sign dinged with importance.

"Hi folks, we're expecting some turbulence for the next two to three minutes, so we ask that everyone remain seated with their seatbelts fastened."

The stewards zoomed throughout the cabin waking any sleepers and making sure everyone had his or her seatbelt fastened. The stewards' flurry of action betrayed their calm faces.

Thunder whipped and cracked; it sounded like God was out to destroy us. Lightning flashed in the sky and lit up thousands of miles of tempestuous clouds all rushing us into the pathway of the deadly lightning demons.

Contact! A lightning bolt seared through the back of our plane.

Even above the exploding gas engines and searing winds, I could still hear the screams of the passengers from the back of the plane as they plummeted to their deaths.

The front of the plane tipped back and we too started to plummet backwards into the water depths far below. I opened my mouth to scream and the sound seemed to race out of my mouth into the heavens. The G-forces must have made me go unconscious.

Suddenly, I was wet. I was freezing. I was alive — for the moment.

I looked around the sinking plane that was quickly taking on water. Most of the passengers were partially in their seatbelts, but were all bloodied and motionless.

"Soldier!" I heard my drill sergeant bark.

I jumped to action as I unhooked my seatbelt as the water rose above my knees. My lower legs were already going numb from the freezing water. I stood and flipped my seat to grab the flotation device. All the people around me were not moving and I knew I had to leave them to their aquatic graves.

I waded to the exit door and tried to release it, but the water pressure was too great. Water was pouring into the ripped fuselage as I waded back through the aisle. The water was above my waist as I grabbed as many flotation devices as I could. I tried to say a prayer or something each time I unhooked someone's seatbelt, rolled him or her away, and took the floatation device. I inflated all the devices and then tied them to each other using people's loose clothing that was floating through the aisles.

The force of the water rushing in through the fuselage was overpowering and I waited until the plane was about two-thirds full of water to make my escape. I thought of my mom, brother, Crystal, and any of the good things I had ever done in my life and took a deep inhale and plunged into the frigid, black water.

I kicked my legs with every bit of strength and pushed towards where the bubbles from the oxygen exiting the plane were traveling towards the surface. My muscles and lungs were burning.

Soldier, push, push!

I broke the surface and inhaled the sweetest air that ever filled my lungs. I quickly maneuvered myself onto my back and propped the upper half of my body on my makeshift raft.

Augh!

Something brushed my legs! It was a shark!

Calm down, soldier!

It was a huge wardrobe, the likes of which I had seen in one of my mother's fashion meetings. It floated and bobbed on the surface. I moved it around so I could reach the latch.

Damn, it was locked. How worthless were fancy clothes at a moment like this!

Soldier, stay focused!

I kept kicking my legs as I tried to grip the sides of the wardrobe to climb on top of it. It kept flipping over and pushing me underwater. I knew I was extending valuable energy and that every movement was leaching precious water from my body.

One last go — I kicked my hardest to propel myself as high as possible onto the wardrobe and slammed by upper body onto its flat surface. I clawed at the farther side of the wardrobe and kicked and kicked the salty water away from me until I was gasping like a fish out of water.

I gathered myself and sat upright to scan the situation. The plane was completely submerged and random suitcases and lifeless bodies popped to the surface to float around and bump into each other.

Goodbye, comrades.

I squinted my eyes to find any signs of life, rescue, or safety. I found the third — I saw a small, tree-covered island just off in the distance.

I grabbed a broken seatback tray table and started to use it as a makeshift paddle, and made my way to my temporary home.

As I approached the island, a light fog enveloped the perimeter. But I could still see that the beach was flora and fauna and luggage — but no other survivors, nada, zero.

I immediately started rummaging through the various suitcases and other objects from the plane. I finally found one suitcase that looked like it was from some type of high-class camping enthusiast. The contents included a cooking pot, rope, blankets, wire, and a strange silver plate.

As I surveyed the objects, I mentally prepared for my survival and escape from the island.

Soldier, do not weigh anchor here.

I fashioned a hammock and a simple tent from the rope and blankets. The fancy plate turned out to be quite cheap so I was able to slowly but surely bend and ultimately break it into several sharp fragments. These became my spears for spearfishing.

I adjusted to life on the island, but I became increasingly agitated as planes flew overhead and cargo steamers chugged away in the far distance.

How could I catch their attention?

I set the snow globe for Crystal on a special log in order to nourish hope that I would see my loved ones again.

But I quickly became the victim of the thoughts that repeatedly burst into my mind.

What is Crystal doing? I'm so thirsty.

How is my mom's business? I'm so hungry.

How are the other soldiers in my unit doing? I'm so thirsty.

What day is it? I'm so hungry.

What ocean am I in? I'm so thirsty.

How can I get more food? I'm so hungry. I'm so thirsty.

I had to get back to my family. I had to get back to life. I caught as many fish and crabs as possible and cut down all the coconuts I could find. This was the last of my fuel and I was going to use it to power out of this island vortex. That sunset, I cooked off and ate the fish and drank the coconut water. When the night turned cool, I wrapped rags around my hands and started my labor.

I kicked, broke, and ripped branches and leaves until my hands bled through rag after rag. At dawn, I ate the last of my food and drank the last of my coconut water as I rewrapped my bleeding hands and started dragging the night's bounty out onto the beach.

I laboriously began to spell "HELP — Plane Crash Survivor!" in the sand.

I set up bonfires on either side of the message to the skies.

Before it had seemed like planes were flying by throughout the day, but now it seemed like only one or two came in an entire day. I had to sleep almost the whole day because of lack of food or water.

All of my muscles were cramping and my hands throbbed as my body struggled to heal itself without any form of medication. I held

Crystal's snow globe and looked at the seemingly pure water that sat inside the glass. I knew it was a false hope of hydration and the globe's water would actually be antifreeze.

Soldier, do not give into this temptation — wait for the real thing.

My eyes closed and I imagined traveling to meet Crystal and begin on our fantastic honeymoon to Paris. My mom would take her to fashion shows and they could go shopping at all the boutiques together. It would be...

A buzz came right into my ear.

Damn flies!

But it was no fly — a low flying plane was coming in close to the sign. I sat up like a bolt and raced to my bonfires. I wildly waved my hands to signal the plane and fell to my knees to grab the flint that was next to the bonfires. Sweat was already beading across my forehead as I struck the flint.

Spark. Spark. Fire! FIRE!

I fanned the flames and ran out to the open part of the beach.

The plane's pilot clearly saw me and dipped its wing in order to signal that rescue was on the way. It turned in the sky and I could see the side door open and things being pushed out of the door and falling down to the beach.

A makeshift care package thudded on the sand. I raced towards it and opened the shirt that had been tied around a few bottles of water and some other dried foods. I could barely use my lacerated hands to open a bottle of water and a package of dried nuts. The water tasted like sweet gold and the salty nuts tasted like salvation.

I sat on the beach laughing, crying, and eating peanuts.

I must have looked weird, but all I could think about was getting back to Crystal and my family.

A little while later a large military helicopter appeared on the horizon and landed on the beach. I was ecstatic to see the robust propellers scatter the remnants of my desperate message.

Within a few hours, I was being wheeled through hospital corridors and looking into the tearful faces of my mom and Crystal.

My mom hugged and kissed me and looked at my hands in dismay as she said, "We never gave up on you. I called in every favor and asked all my friends to use their private planes to keep searching for you."

Crystal never let go of my arm as she explained, "I flew to Paris to work with your mother to find you. I love you so much and I could never imagine my life without you."

That evening, the doctors said that I was healthy, but dehydrated and malnourished. Of course, I needed antibiotics to help heal my hands as well as several stitches in particularly bad places. But I had survived an entire month alone on a deserted island and had returned to the land of the living.

The next day, my hospital was noisy with journalists who wanted to publish my story. I just made a simple statement out in front of the hospital and then my mom, Crystal, and I drove back to my mom's Paris home.

The next morning, I turned on the television and realized that I had become some kind of celebrity as I heard international reports about my rescue: *Veteran Survived a Plane CRASH and Rescued a Month Later.*

As I listened to the reports about myself, I found myself walking to and from the refrigerator over and over again as I drank and ate to my heart's content. But I only felt full when I had Crystal in my arms.

14

What Lives in the Walls

By

Jorge Gonzalez

I was just a shy, young Mexican guy who was about to turn fifteen and about to start a new high school. My old city was notorious for gangs, corruption, and racism; but this new city was notorious for missing people.

Surprisingly, most people were friendly to me because they thought I was something different. But of course, some people feared my own ghetto background and thought that I would be a tough guy.

I made a few friends and made my way through classes until I became the target of the school ace football player named Brad. He was like a silent cat who would just show up out of nowhere with his steroid muscles. He always seemed to be in my face.

"What do you want with me?" I asked him nervously.

"Why were you talking to me ex-girlfriend, huh? I didn't like the way you were looking at her," he grunted.

My mind raced through the morning's events. Oh, that's right; it must have been the cheerleader who wanted me to massage her shoulders. I knew it was too good to be true. She must have been using me to bait him and make him jealous. I could feel a sheen of cold sweat forming on my upper lip.

Had he seen us? If I say something and he had not seen us, then that might even be worse. What can I do? This guy wants to beat the sh*t out of someone and it might just be me.

Just then, his ex-girlfriend pounced on the scene and shouted, "Brad! Leave the kid alone, you Neanderthal!"

I stood paralyzed by all the commotion and my mind jumped to thoughts of Maria — yeah, she was the whole reason I was even at that crazy school.

Maria. Maria? Why was the name Maria coming into my mind?

I backed away from Brad and the cheerleader, who seemed to be really amping up into a fight.

What was the name of the cheerleader? I always seemed to be in a daze lately.

Somehow I stumbled home in a daze and pushed open the front door to hear my mom ask, "Jorge, did you see Maria at school today?"

"No," I lied.

Wait, had I seen Maria that day?

"This is your mission, Jorge," she added. "You must meet with her."

My mission?

I did not eat dinner or do any homework as I just fell asleep on top of my bed covers.

Maria flitted in and out of my restless dreams and then appeared in the flesh before me the next day at school. I do not know how I knew what her face looked like, but I immediately recognized her, even though she was older. She had grown into a beautiful woman, especially her twins (*wink, wink*).

"Why have I been transferred to this school?" I asked her as we cascaded through the hallways.

We passed a bulletin board that had pictures of several missing people.

She leaned into my ear and whispered, "We are now part of the first cell division and need to get our further instructions in the gym. There we'll find out which organization we've been assigned to."

"Organization?" I asked with a wrinkled brow, as we pushed open the swinging doors to the empty gym.

"Don't you know what we're doing?" she asked and peered into my face.

"I forgot. I don't know. Everything is so different here," I weakly replied.

"Follow me," she sternly responded as she firmly planted her hand on my back and pushed me towards a dark hallway at the back of the gym.

We stood in the dark and Maria pressed herself close to me.

I was uncomfortable and confused.

"Do you remember our mission?" she said intensely.

"Yes," I said. "It's to destroy the negative energy that flows around our people," I automatically replied in a monotone that surprised me.

"Your memory is coming back," Maria said with confidence and optimism.

I had no idea what was really happening, but I knew something was happening.

Maria walked me to school every day and taught me about my latent powers and how to use my abilities for the greater good.

I was concentrating on moving a stone with my mind when a voice startled me out of my task.

"Hey, are you staring at that rock?" a girl's voice asked me.

I blinked and focused on the girl in front of me — it was the cheerleader who had thrown me in Brad's way and the one who had saved me.

"Um, sorry 'bout the other day with that stupid turd. He's my ex-boyfriend. He's all bark and no bite, so just ignore him. He doesn't really beat people up," she explained.

I shrugged as if it were no big deal. I smiled inside as I thought about how I could probably rain down a hailstorm of rocks on Brad's meathead with my rediscovered abilities.

"By the way, my name is Sarah Waiters. Aren't you Jorge?" she asked.

But I was quickly dragged away from the charming Sarah by the brusque hand of Maria.

Strangely angry, Maria said, "My perverted sister is coming into our squad."

Personally, I didn't know about her having a sibling — let alone a "perverted" one.

"We're in a squad?" I asked in confusion, as we stood under a tree alone.

"Durr," Maria said sarcastically.

Maria launched into a long dictation about the number of squads in our territory and that this should all be common sense. As she berated me for not knowing this secret information, all her words went in one of my ears and out the other. I was smitten with Sarah, who was practicing her cheering routines with her own squad of beautiful girls.

A sucker punch to the jaw pulled me out of my reverie as Maria brought my back from the world of jumping cheerleaders to the world of moving rocks with my mind.

I rubbed my jaw — yeah, I deserved a hit, but not one that hard.

I walked uneasily next to the fuming Maria as we made our way home. Boy, she was in a bad mood and I was just about to find out why, as a voluptuous girl appeared on the sidewalk in front of us.

It was clear that she and Maria knew each other. It was clear that this was Maria's "perverted" sister, as she hugged me in a hello that someone involved my unintentionally motor boating her. I was surprised but happy. This day was getting better and better.

Again, I got a punch from Maria. It was worth it.

"Sis, why'd you do that? You big jerk," Maria accosted the buxom girl who laughed.

"Thank you for the service," I said to my new friend as I created an old-fashioned bow.

This earned me another punch from Maria. Again, it was worth it.

All this merriment came to an abrupt stop — a violet purple aura of negativity washed across the three of us.

"It's almost here," Maria said softly in a terrified voice.

Everything started to feel strange and we all fainted and fell to the ground.

I opened my eyes and struggled to move around.

Where was I?

I was neatly tucked into my own bed.

I pulled my hands out from under the tight bed sheet and grabbed my phone to text Maria to figure out what had happened.

"Let's meet face-to-face," she texted back.

I just did not know what to make of things as I stumbled along to her house where she swung open the door and hugged me.

"Yay! We finished our very first mission!" she said with glee.

I still felt confused because I thought we were going to be in trouble since we had fainted and I did not think we had actually accomplished anything. I did not know what to say, but I just smiled as if I knew that we had been successful. I always felt one step behind the eight ball in this city.

A few weeks later, I got a disturbing phone call from my friend Jordan who had been a cop for a while. Recently, I had noticed that she had been acting sullen and distant.

Over the phone, her voice sounded muffled as she revealed, "I've been so distracted for the past weeks because I got a dispatch call about a late-night break in at a local church."

I did not know why this break in would be so troubling to her because she had dealt with all sorts of crimes in her career. Something was clearly different about this situation.

I could sense her gripping the phone as she relayed the story to me, "When my partner and I got to the church, two people were waiting outside for us. It was a middle-aged woman in a suit and an older man in a priest's vestments. They were clearly agitated and they were constantly scanning the surroundings. The man was focused on some broken glass that they'd found around the side of the church. He told me that no one was supposed to be there that late at night, so they knew it wasn't just some kind of accident."

I let all this register as I mentally envisioned these two people who seemed so otherworldly.

"I don't want to talk about this over the phone anymore," she abruptly said.

"Do you want to meet?" I asked with concern.

"Let's meet at El Camino," she said and hung up the phone.

I stared at the phone in confusion.

Was this the same Jordan who had survived a shootout and any number of other crazy police calls? Why was she asking me to meet her at a bar? I was underage.

I pulled on my jacket and made my way the few blocks to the bar.

When I opened the door, the stale smell of cheap beer and lost dreams wove themselves into my psyche.

A hand shot up in the air as Jordan called me over to a table in the back.

"What do you want?" she said with a mild slur.

I wondered if she had been drinking at home as I casually said I would have a Coke.

"Suit yourself," she answered as she stood and walked to the bar.

The barkeep was drying glasses and quietly chatting with an obviously long-time customer. He did not even flinch as Jordan reached across the bar to grab the bottle of Jack Daniels and a bottle of Coke.

Back at the table, she set the Coke in front of me and poured herself and took a shot of the JD.

I wondered if she had seen something terrible — the kind of things that scars people's minds and they just live on as ghosts of themselves. She seemed like a paper-thin version of her previous self.

"What happened at the church?" I gently asked Jordan who started pouring herself another shot.

Luckily, she just seemed bent on sipping this one.

"What did you see there?" I asked with more intensity.

She looked back at me with her quickly reddening eyes and took a huge breath.

"You know my partner Jim?" she asked.

"Sure," I responded. "Is this still about the church break in?"

She nodded and started talking as if the conversation had never paused, "We started walking around the whole area near the two strangers. I realized that it wasn't just like a regular church. It was more like a compound with several different buildings. The different buildings seemed to have signs saying one building was a cafeteria or a preschool. It was like a miniature city."

"One huge building had stained glass windows that had all been broken and shattered," she added.

"Do you think it was a hate crime?" I asked.

"Ha," she guffawed with a strange twinge of cynicism as she finished that shot.

"Jim had called for backup and two more officers arrived with a canine unit. The dog had to be pulled along at every step and kept its tail between its legs as it sniffed out the area," she added.

Everything was getting stranger and stranger. I knew I had not had a drop of liquor, but I was starting to feel woozy.

"What don't they show on TV?" I asked.

Jordan darkly laughed and continued, "The officers and I went into the building with the broken glass and I grabbed a broom to sweep up the glass so the dog wouldn't cut its paws. But the dog just stayed at the door and had to be pulled past the doorjamb once the glass was cleared."

I shivered at the thought of this dog struggling against being pulled inside.

"I shined my flashlight all around the interior of the church. It was pristine white and so clean you could lick off the floor. It seemed like a sterile mental institution," she said as she filled the shot glass again.

The fumes from the liquor burned in my nostrils.

"Then I saw it — the fatal funnel," she said with an odd flourish. She seemed to be getting into her own storytelling and leaving the vibe of horror she had started out with.

"Fatal funnel?" I asked with an unexpected slur.

"The fatal funnel — a long entryway with no escape route. If something comes at you, you have nowhere to dive or hide," she said.

"Something?" I asked.

"The two other officers, the dog, and Jim and I fanned out through the space and tried to check every inch of the place for hiding intruders," she continued.

"Do you think someone was hiding in there?" I asked.

With this she looked me dead in the eye and said, "There was an odd smell to the whole place. It was industrial and chemical. It was familiar but none of us could identify it. The dog seemed more at ease and kept happily sniffing around, but never made an alert. Honestly, I started to think it was even stranger that the dog was now at ease."

I looked around the bar and it seemed that everyone was looking at us through slits in their eyes — like they were monitoring us.

Jordan looked intently at me and continued, "We went through silent room after silent room. We checked behind their weird altar. I don't even know what religion they were supposed to be. The strange smell would get stronger and weaker in different spots. God, it makes me want to puke just thinking about that smell," she said with a grimace and poured another shot down her throat.

I could not even understand how she could be drinking this much and still be sitting upright. I could not understand where her story was going. The apprehension was sickening.

"Finally, we found a ladder that seemed to lead up to an attic. The smell was so strong. Jim the rookie went up first and checked everywhere. It was the last place and there was no one. The other officers and Jim started to exit the building. The dog seemed to be drowsy. But you know, I'm always afraid that I'll tell people that they're all safe and then some jerk is hiding in the shadows. So, I held back and..."

Jordan jumped across the table and grabbed my shoulders and looked me square in the face.

"...ha ha ha. You should see your face," she mocked.

"What's wrong with you?" I asked like an angry sleepwalker who has been startled awake by the nightmare of reality.

"Suddenly, this huge guy jumps out of the shadows. I tackled him," Jordan said as she mimed the wrestling.

"Was he the guy who broke in?" I asked again with a stronger sense of focus.

Jordan seemed to take everything so seriously again and had another full shot. I looked at the half empty bottle and thought about her stomach becoming the new bottle for the liquor.

"He just kept babbling about being punished for his sins. Jim and I had to cuff him in order just to get him to calm down. We finally got his butt on the floor and he lapsed into a confused silence. But in the calm, I realized that the chemical smell was strongest from the direction he had run from," she said.

I really felt like everyone in the bar was pretending that they were not listening to us when in reality they were hanging on every one of her words.

"Jim and I left the babbling man on the floor and followed the smell towards a long hallway. At the end, it seemed like some sort of a fake wall had been scratched and punched through. We shone our lights down the hallway and the smell was just burning up our noses. But then I noticed beeping sounds like you hear at hospitals. Beep…Beep…Beep…"

"Just get on with it! What did you see?" I said in frustration.

Jordan looked at me keenly and asked, "You sure you want to know, kid?"

"Just get on with it," I muttered.

"There were all these medical machines and tubes and IV drips with fluids that were all different colors. All the tubes seemed to be feeding into this huge block of cement that was like white plaster," she explained and took a shot filled to the brim. "And that's when I noticed the fingers sticking out of the plaster."

"The fingers?"

Jordan nodded with a grimace and continued, "You know all the missing people. That's where they are. Ha, mystery solved. Just can't tell anybody about it."

"The people?" I just could not wrap my head around it.

"Yeah, you stupid kid," she flared with anger. "Some nut job's been kidnapping people and keeping them alive in the concrete wall. That's what all the fluids and machines were for. He wasn't trying to kill them. He was keeping them alive. I don't know what he was doing," she said as she slumped back into her seat.

"Who's he?"

She ignored my question but leaned in real serious to me, "I'm not allowed to tell anyone. But you're just a kid. You'll keep my secret, won't you? Who would believe you anyway?"

"What about Jim and the other cops? What about the middle-aged lady and the priest?"

"Who knows if that guy was a priest! I don't think priests are supposed to stab police officers."

"Stab?"

"Yeah, I told you already. When I found the other police officer, he said the priest had stabbed him," she said in annoyance.

"You never told me that," I said back in annoyance.

"You gotta try to keep up kid. No one will ever see that lady or that priest again. Well, I bet some unlucky fools will meet the two of them," she added sadly.

I wondered if she was going to cry. Everything had become so heavy. I could barely breathe.

"The EMTs came but they couldn't just pull the people out of the concrete wall. So, we had to have engineers all come and delicately get them out of the wall. It looked like one of the archeological digs, except the tomb was upright. Each person looked worse than the last. They were like emaciated corpses and their skin was all burned from the chemicals. Their burns were leaking horrendous fluids," she added with a frown.

I did not know where I was anymore. *Was I still in the bar?*

"Kid, just imagine. All those people being tortured for years in that wall all right under the feet of children attending Sunday school," she said, as she seemed to look right through me.

"I thought you said you didn't know what type of church it was?" I asked in confusion.

"I don't know what the whole thing was. I don't know anything about anything anymore. You know, the physical details all just seem like a distant horror movie to me. But you know what keeps me awake at night," Jordan said as she downed yet another shot. "It's those last two captives who had been in there the longest."

"How long had they been in the wall?" I asked.

"Each person had been in there for different amounts of time. The ones who had only been in there for a few months or only a year or two were all so grateful to be released," Jordan answered.

"Only a year or two?" I asked in a drowsy voice.

"But the last two captives had each been in there for eighteen and twenty-years. This is what haunts me — the last two captives," Jordan paused to look around the room.

"What?"

"The last two…," she said as she shook her head.

"What about them?"

Jordan downed the last of her beer and looked me dead in eye as she said, "They begged to be put back in the wall."

She shook her head as she wiped her mouth with the back of her hand.

I kept staring at her, but everything was becoming hazy like a mirage. I could not seem to put two thoughts together as I watched Jordan stumble out of the bar.

I died four days later.

I do not know how I ended up in the wall or if it was that I was back in the wall.

15

Leondes Moon

By

Augustin Jara

My name is Leondes Moon — Leo for short — and this is the story about how I reached the place I am at right now.

It all started about two and a half years ago when I was in the eighth grade. I was a typical Latino living in Watts, CA, where everybody just calls it L.A. I did not stand out from the crowd with my brown hair and black eyes. I was another average height, skinny dude who loved his sports.

But I soon found my true love. It was a small, middle school called College Ready that was designed to push students on to better lives. I knew something was different on the first day when we got tablets and I made to the end of the day without getting into a fistfight. I realized that the classrooms were not just sterile, anonymous rooms, but were more like living rooms in homes where a family of teachers nurtured the students.

I not only learned from my successes at College Ready, but also from my failures.

History nearly proved to be my Waterloo as I failed the final two times, which prompted Ms. Johnson to chastise me, "Leo, if you don't straighten up your act, you're going to end up like one of those bums on the street gripping a brown paper bag like his life depended on it. Do you want to be one of those guys?"

For a second, I could feel my hand squeezing onto the rough crinkling of a brown paper bag wrapped around the neck of a bottle of cheap, piss-yellow beer.

That talk changed my life. I would never be one of those guys whose images became the motivational posters lining the insides of my mind.

Even though I was motivated to study and knew the alternative if I failed, I still struggled with my grades. My scores fluctuated, but I always managed to bounce back until:

Dear Mr. and Mrs. Moon,

While Leondes' teachers see that he works hard in his classes, Leondes is in danger of failing the eighth grade and being expelled from our school. We would like to hold a parent-teacher conference to discuss the next steps for his academic career.

Sincerely,

Dr. Locke, Principal of C. R.

I revolted against this fate and I swore, "F*ck! Not this! Not now! I'm going to get beat!"

I took my time walking home as my mind wondered how my mom would react. She had warned me about my grades and I knew that they would have already called her about the situation. I sauntered and wandered the whole way home and stopped to look in every shop window. I had no time and no money; but I wanted to preserve the last bubble of happiness before the inevitable chewing out that I would get once I got home.

As I pushed open the front door I heard that inevitable calling of my name as my mother said, "Leo, get in here. The school called about your grades."

But when I rounded the kitchen corner, I was surprised that her face looked more sad than angry.

"Leo, your uncle Pepe died two hours ago," she sighed. "His final words were about you," she added.

This was weird. I was too shocked to even react.

She put the kitchen dish towel on the refrigerator door handle and said in a wistful tone, "Pepe said, 'Leo, make it big.' It was like he was talking to you as if you were right in front of him."

I could feel this deep frown growing on my face as tears welled up in my eyes. My mentor had died — my sweet Uncle Pepe's funeral was on Friday. Nothing else was important anymore.

I castigated myself incessantly — it should have been me who died! He deserved to live while I just wasted my opportunities.

I did not sleep, eat, shower, or do any schoolwork.

My teachers understood that grief had gripped my soul and gave me a reprieve in my homework and extensions on my exams.

But now, I had the greatest trial of my life — my uncle's funeral loomed in the upcoming future. Friday marched inexorably towards me as I found myself sleep-walking into the church where his funeral was being held.

The stained glass windows showed Jesus dying on the cross and other windows showed a lamb sitting in the paws of a gentle lion. The sunlight glanced off the funerary calla lilies whose suffocating fragrance permeated the worship hall.

A white man in a black priest frock presided over the ceremony. I stood, kneeled, and sat whenever the people around me did so. I could not even hear what the people or the priest were saying about my dear uncle.

As the funeral ended and the pallbearers hoisted my uncle's casket on their shoulders, I followed my weeping mother into the church aisle to walk behind the casket. They were taking my uncle to be cremated so that we could put him on top of an Aztec pyramid as his final resting place.

Outside the church, the pallbearers slid my uncle's casket into the hearse as all the family women daubed their eyes and noses with handkerchiefs. I was about to be overcome with tears when a strong hand grasped my shoulder. I turned to see my cousin Victor.

"Hey, don't look so glum. He had a great life and he loved you so much. He'd hate how sad everyone is. You know how he liked for everyone to be happy," Victor said.

I stifled my sobs as he added, "The dead may no longer be with us, but they can always see us."

When I got home, I planned just to collapse on my bed and sleep. But I was surprised to see an Xbox 360 on my bed. There was a card from my cousin Victor that read:

Dear Cuz,

I know the loss of my dad, your uncle, has been a terrible blow to everyone. This is a little gift from my mom and me to help you forget about the loss. There are three games: Black Ops 1, Assassin's Creed

2, and Hitman. Have fun, cousin. I'm here for you, come, and I hope

you come to visit us.

> *Best,*

> *Victor*

I rubbed my face and I could feel the streaks of tears that had

dried into salty lines that ran down my face. I went to the bathroom

and washed my face.

How could I play games when my uncle was dead?

I read Victor's note again and slowly opened the Xbox and

hooked up the console. Those were my last moments of slowness and

of reality. I was quickly absorbed into the gaming world of fantasy

and control where the dead simply arise to fight again at the push of a

button. I waged vicious wars on my enemies, as my avatars grew

more and more fearsome.

The weekend passed in a blur and Monday seemed like it existed

in a different dimension from the previous Friday's funeral.

"Leo, get up. It's time to go," my mother called.

I did my usual morning routine and then went to the kitchen. Everything seemed so faded, slow, and weak after my foray into the alternate Xbox reality.

I watched my mother sipping her coffee as I poured milk into my cereal.

"Please, try to make a good impression today," my mother said.

"What? Why," I asked with a mouthful of Raisin Bran.

"You remember, you got the school notice about your new teacher. This might be your last chance. This is about your whole future now," she said and looked directly at me.

I just looked down at my cereal and nodded.

I did not remember anything about a new teacher or a new class or anything. All I remembered was thrashing the Ottoman Empire in Assassin's Creed.

My walk to school was arduous and I felt like I had not used my muscles for ages.

When I finally found my new classroom, I was nearly late.

"Well, hello. You must be Leo. I'm Ms. Luiz," my new teacher introduced herself.

I nodded as I glanced around the classroom. My eyes rested on a beautiful girl with shiny hair that cascaded like a waterfall down her back. She smiled at me.

Who was that and why was she smiling at me?

"Leo, are you still there?" Ms. Luiz said in a lighthearted tone.

Embarrassed, I pulled myself together and nodded yes.

"Good, before you sit down, can you tell me something about yourself?" she asked.

"Well, I'm a football player, and I like to read," I responded.

She was clearly caught off guard by the second half of my sentence and smiled brightly.

She turned her attention to the class and asked, "Would anyone like to help Leo catch up?"

A hand shot up in the air.

"I would, Ms. Luiz," a girl, whose name I would learn was Emily, said with alacrity.

Emily soon became my angel as she helped me with every class that we had together. She spent time with me, getting the required research books from the library, and she photocopied all her old notes and handouts for me to study. By the end of the school year, we had already been dating for three months and my grades had dramatically improved.

I heard the 3 pm bell ring, signaling the end of another day as the overhead speaker crackled to life for the vice-principal to make announcements and to list off the offenders destined for afterschool detention.

I grabbed my backpack and nonchalantly headed to my locker.

"Leondes Moon, please come to the principal's office," the vice-principal's voice stopped me dead in my tracks.

What was this about?

I made my way through the crowded hallways of teenagers busting to begin their afternoons of their real lives that existed outside of school.

In the cool of the principal's office, I sat dumbfounded by the entire meeting.

"Son, we found this in your locker," principal said as he held out a huge bag that looked like it contained several ounces of weed.

"Sir, that's not mine. I stopped using any drugs and have not seen or used any weed for ages," I replied, as I looked him in the eye hoping that he would feel my sincerity.

"Well, the teachers say that you have missed a lot of classes lately."

"Yes, that's true," I admitted. "I've been studying a lot outside of class with my girlfriend. I'm sorry for that, but I'm clean. You can test me."

"Son, there's nothing we can do at this point. You've missed too many classes and now you've been caught with drugs. We have no choice but to expel you," he gravely added.

"But my graduation — I've worked so hard!" I stammered.

I rushed out of the room and my heart slowed with every step as I replayed every word over and over again in my mind. I made my way to the outside fields where I looked with sadness at the middle schoolers running and playing outside.

They did not even know about how disappointing life could be!

I looked to the skies as I saw gray clouds gathering and could hear thunder rolling towards the city. It was like the skies were outwardly expressing my devastated soul. As the heavy raindrops fell to earth, the students all scrambled back inside.

In between the splattering raindrops, I could hear the last words between myself and the principal.

"Leo, come back here. We're not done," he had said.

"I am, though," I had responded with a bitterness that I did not know dwelled inside me.

Grief and shock haunted me in the weeks after my uncle's death. I stood in the rain asking questions of why, what, when, how, and who. The questions endlessly played in my addled mind.

The biggest question that plagued me concerned how the teachers had even gotten my locker code.

I stood outside in the rain as the bitter drops hit my face like cold crystals cutting a thousand tiny cuts into my flesh. I did not seek shelter even as the thunder roared in the sky and the lightning threatened to ignite the surrounding trees.

One bold lightning bolt flashed to the ground just a few feet from me, but I could have cared less. They had taken everything I had worked so hard to create for my future.

Across the field, I saw my girl with some guy. But she did not see me as I slowly approached them. As I neared, I realized that the guy was rumored to be the newest drug delivery guy in our school. I hid under the bleachers so I could listen and watch them.

"Here is the money we promised you," my girl said.

I was furious. I stepped out to confront them as the rain obscured the tears that fell from my eyes.

"How could you do this to me? I believed you were trying to help me!" I stammered as the thunder and lightning intensified. "Why are you ruining a kid's dreams?"

"Look, son…," the drug dealer started to say.

"Do not call me *son*," I fumed.

"Leo, listen. It's not what it looks like," pleaded Emily.

"What?" I shouted in disbelief. "I guess you want me to believe that the drugs that the administrators found just accidentally fell into my bags just as I find you with this dealer?"

The lighting danced around us and hit a trash can three feet from us. The can shot up into the air like a rocket. But I was not distracted as I kept my eyes glued to Emily and the dealer. The last thing I remember as the trash can made contact with my head before returning to earth was Emily asking for forgiveness.

Two weeks later, I woke up from my comma. From my hospital bed, I looked to the tray table beside me to notice a diploma and a letter that read:

Congrats, Leo. You've graduated eighth grade with one of the highest GPAs.

I was flabbergasted, but thrilled.

When I was healthy again, my mom drove me home from the hospital and took me for a special shopping spree at GameStop, where I got Black Ops 1 and 2, Assassin Creed: Black Flag, and G.T.A 5. The food that I ate when I left the hospital was the best food ever — a burger, chili cheese fries, and a root beer. I remember the hot cheese oozing from the fries that I stuffed in my mouth and the juicy taste of the burger with lettuce, tomato, and ranch dressing.

At home, I got some posole with lime and chili with tapatio. I could not believe that I was still hungry, but I realized I was hungry for more than just food. As I took my first spoonful, I was flooded with the flavors of home as the soup's corn chips crunched in my mouth. As I finished the posole, I felt contemplative as I thought about all the things that had happened in my life and how I wanted to have more control over my future.

I said all these strong things to myself when I was fresh from the hospital. But these types of things are hard to do in real life.

First, I ended up getting involved in a fight my brother had with some neighborhood guys. My brother had kept getting into trouble with some people who should not be messed with and things were coming to a head. As I walked the streets with my brother, we turned to a neighborhood where everything became eerily quiet. There was no a sound or a soul around. I knew something was terribly wrong.

"Bro, let's go back," I urged my brother.

"No, man. I need the money," my brother said.

"Something's wrong. Let's go back."

"Ok, I feel it, too."

But it was too late as we were suddenly surrounded by two guys in front of us and three guys behind us. All of them wore masks and all of them meant business.

"Where you going?" sneered one of them.

"Home," I replied.

One of the other guys took a swing at me and smacked my face. I hit the pavement and rolled over to look up at the sky.

If I can look up, I can get up. You were raised to fight or die trying.

I mustered all my strength and pulled myself to a standing position and raised my fists to battle these masked hooligans. My brother joined me in battle and we took each of those guys down. Our faces were bruised and swollen, but we had finished the job.

When my brother and I returned home, we both faced a litany of shouts from my family who were worried about our safety — especially mine since I had been in the coma. My brother and I knew we would get into even more trouble if we tried to explain how the whole thing had started. So, we just suffered their concerned anger and went to our rooms when they finally tired of admonishing us.

Two days later, my face still looked like a punching bag. Honestly, I could not believe I had survived such a fight, but there I was holding my own in this crazy life.

I went over to Collin's house to see what he was up to.

From the hallway, I heard the unmistakable voices shouting through a great battle.

"Take cover!"

"Man down!"

"He's bleeding out!"

"What's the evac time?"

"5mics out!"

"Air strike! Hit the floor!"

"Augh! Help, my legs!"

"Shut up! We need help!"

"Keep on running!"

I opened the door to his room and saw the familiar glare of the video game screen. The battle looked so realistic in the HD 1480.

"Welcome, bro," Collins said as he passed me a control panel.

I sat in the chair and quickly entered the world of war where I was in complete control of my destiny and had all the power in the world.

This day imbued me with a sense of power that I could not drag myself away from. From then on, I became immersed in binge-playing and would spend days playing. The upcoming fall school year seemed eons away.

Even though I was an indestructible force in the game world, I was reminded once again of the frailty of human life. I still have nightmares about what happened.

It was around midnight and I was walking home with my homie Collin. It had been a cool, peaceful night of perfect partying. Collin had actually worn a suit to the party, which was a hoity-toity affair (certainly by Watts's standards). They had imported beer and wine and the women were gorgeous.

But it was a strange party and the whole night had had a strange vibe to it. I was tagging along with Collin and this girl he had picked up at the party. Our homes were near each other, so I just planned to go to my house. Then, a strange car slowed and the passenger rolled down the window.

I was hammered and I thought he might be asking for directions. Suddenly, bullets went flying.

The three of us screamed and I tried to duck behind a parked car. Collin and the girl ducked behind another car. Shots rang out as the shooters emptied their barrels. The stench of gunpowder was replaced by the acrid smell of burnt rubber as the car peeled away.

"Collin, where you at?" I shouted in the stillness.

"Over here," I heard him weakly reply.

I ran to my homie Collin and saw that he had been shot several times in the chest and legs.

My mind reeled with confused anger.

Why is this happening? Collin is so young!

I quickly knelt down to hold Collin, who spit blood as I raised his head, "Bro it's cold. Ha ha ha…"

"Don't talk, man."

"It's game over for me, man. See you later."

I could register that the girl was screaming, but everything remained silent for me. She started running down the street to find some real safety. I laid my own bullet-ridden body next to my dead homie. The last thing I remember was the paramedics telling me that I had been shot in the arm and the thigh as they hoisted me into the ambulance.

A week after I left the hospital, Collin was buried with his Xbox and his football in a grave next to his grandfather. I bitterly noted how death had skipped a generation and taken a grandson before his time. Back at Collin's house, I did not talk to anyone and I just silently accepted the gift of Collin's game control that had all his dates on the back. I did not even look at it, let alone play it, for weeks.

Everything seemed so meaningless as people around me seemed to be dying and other people betrayed me. I felt that there was no reason to make an effort in this violent, illogical world.

One day, I was getting the mail and I saw that I had received a mysterious letter from Collin. I opened it and read through it.

Dear Agustin,

If you're reading this, it's because I am dead. I knew it was coming because the doctor told me that I have heart cancer and that I only have two weeks to live. I wrote this letter to tell you that the sky's the limit. The world of videogames are just pretend and memories. You must make your own real paradise. Take this letter as a goodbye from me and take my control that is in the third cabinet. It's made especially for you. I put the key to my room in this letter so everyone will know that I wanted you to have the control.

Thanks for the fun times,

Collin, your homie

I did not know how to react to the letter. So, I just grabbed the key to his room and headed to his house. His mom was upset at the thought of opening Collin's room because she was not emotionally prepared to see all his things again. But she was a strong woman and relented.

I opened the door and sunlight flooded the dusty room. I could see the Black Ops 2 sitting inside the Xbox 360 package and I could smell the sticky-sweet blue soda and the stale corndogs left from our last gaming session.

The memories of our times together flooded my mind and my eyes teared up. But I took a deep breath and started to look for the control in the cabinet. Sure enough, he had put my name on the front of the control that was all decked out in black and gold. But I noticed something next to the control. It was his chain. I held it in my hands and knew that Collin would always be an important part of my life.

Collin had given me more than just the gifts of the control and the chain — he had reignited a sense of purpose and motivation in my life. And school was around the corner. I was not prepared at all as my mind ran over all the problems that were plaguing my life.

I had to take a last break from reality and I immersed myself with the world of Black Ops 1 and 2. I went on to finish half of Assassin's Creed: Brotherhood. Then, I went into the world of The Walking Dead. All of these hours of battle training trained my mind to be a strong person who can handle any difficulty and can find a solution to any problem.

I was as ready as I would ever be for ninth grade at the huge Lock High School, which was bigger than my previous school. I had no idea that I was about to meet a teacher who would truly change my life — Ms. Hope.

Of course, at first I thought she was just another teacher who was just there for a paycheck and their own summer vacations. But I realized that this white, blue-eyed teacher with blond hair actually cared about her students. She was not afraid of the older students and treated everyone fairly and tried to really encourage them to shoot for their dreams.

She did not just treat us like hood people, instead she treated us like people who deserved a chance to go to college and that we could make it there. She openly talked about how there was so much more to life than just drugs, liquor, and women.

She took special care to help me fix up my act. I still had reservations about her until one day she did something that dispelled any doubts.

"Ms. Hope? What are you doing here?" I asked her from inside my house porch screen early one morning when I was getting a slow start to the day.

"I told you that if you come late again, I would pick you up at your house. Your mom said it was okay," she brightly said.

"I guess," I said with some confusion and trepidation.

Since that day, she helped me do better in school and she helped me translate my videogame skills to the real world. I learned how to strategize and how to persevere, as life itself is a battle sometimes. Ms. Hope prepared me for tenth grade and for life. Now, I plan to pursue a college degree and to take care of my new lady love, who has shown me the way to live a happy life in the hard world. I have seen death, but I have also seen life.

16

Assassin

By

Miguel Lara

When sleeping, the mind goes into a world where anything can happen because everything is all in the mind and dreams become the reality. These thoughts filtered through my mind as I was in the midst of dying.

Suddenly, I came across the memory of a dream I had had years ago. I remembered having the dream like it was yesterday and I remember the reality of the dream as if it were yesterday.

In that realm, I was an eighteen-year-old retired assassin who lived with his younger brother and mother in a small town in Los Angeles.

"Mother, where are the clothes that I washed," I yelled to my mom who was in the other room.

"They're on the couch where you left them yesterday when you got home," she calmly told me.

Today was an important day because it was my one-year anniversary with my girlfriend Abby.

"Thanks, Mother," I said as I ran downstairs to grab the clothes.

I took a quick shower, got dressed, put on my backpack, and rushed to my car with my keys in my hand.

As I pulled into the school parking lot, I spied my girlfriend standing by the gate waiting for me. I kept my eye on her as I parked my car — she seemed preoccupied. I wondered if she thought I had forgotten our anniversary. I walked over to her and leaned over to hug and kiss her.

She seemed cold.

"Are you okay, princess?" I asked. "Did something happen?" I added.

"It's over," she said with a blank face and a resolute tone.

I felt the whole world collapse on top of me. I stood paralyzed as the love of my life walked away from me as if I had meant nothing to her. Tears welled in my eyes and I brushed them away as I composed myself.

I glanced down at my phone to realize that it had been ringing for quite some time. It was a familiar number, but one that I had not seen for quite some time. I needed to move to a more private space before I could answer.

"How did you get this new number?" I asked with suspicion.

"It's not too hard to find you, Agent A," the man on the phone said. "How's life been treating you?" he asked.

"It has its ups and downs. Nothing I can't handle," I answered.

"Have been keeping your skills sharp, Agent A?" he asked.

I knew this was not just a social call and I knew that things were taking a turn for the worse.

"It's a good job for a good pay out. It'll just take a bit of your time," he cajoled.

"If it's such an easy job, why is the pay so high?" I asked.

The phone went silent for about thirty seconds, and then I heard him say, "Will you be able to do the job? I'll explain the details later."

I knew that I really did not have a choice in these matters and answered, "I'll do it."

"I'll send to pick you up," he responded and hung up the phone.

I returned to my day, which ended up being a living hell. The whole day people kept asking me what was going on between Abby and me. It came as a shock to a lot of people because my girlfriend and I were always so close. Nobody saw it coming, nobody...

When the day's hell was over, I went home. The guy from the phone call was waiting for me at the door of my home. When I saw him, I didn't say a word. I just gave him a look that meant for him to follow me so we could talk in private. I led him to a rundown park where we sat undisturbed on a bench.

"So, Agent A, can you do the job?" he asked me as he ran his hand through his gelled black hair.

He jabbed his stubby index finger at me as he added, "The job pays two million, by the way."

"Who's the target?" I asked.

"It is a teacher who's been doing illegal things in his spare time."

"I'll do it," I said as I stood and walked away.

Many thoughts raced through my head. I breathed deeply and returned to my training to always keep a clear mind before doing anything too big.

That night, I went to sleep in my bed in my home. But when I awoke, I was not in my home — I was in the training ground where I had learned to be an assassin. My sword that I had not seen for many moons beckoned me from its place of honor on the mantle.

"I have missed you, Justification!" I bowed my head in greeting to my weapon, the Katana sword that had been given to me by a very old, wise man. Justification had a reputation that it could kill anyone with a beating heart in just a single, well-positioned strike.

As I picked up the sword, all the training that was deep in my mind returned and I was back to being an assassin. I had been the best assassin while I was growing up in the organization, where I had lived for as long as I could remember. I had left when I turned seventeen because I had found a reason to stay alive and not be killed — Abby.

But now, that reason had evaporated and my old life took over. As I held the sword in my hand a simulation exercise activated. Fifteen foes appeared out of thin air as they took battle positions on the mat in front of me.

A voice over the intercom boomed, "Kill these adversaries in less than fifteen minutes…"

I can do it in under five.

"…and make it to the platform on the other side of the training area."

This might be just a little harder than I thought.

As I heard the instructions, I noticed that little timer in my eye line. I was startled and looked around, but I realized that the timer was being projected through my own eyesight. No time to revel in technology. The clock was counting down and I was just standing there.

I ignored the clock and immediately, calmly started battle attack. I dragged my sword behind me as I walked toward one of my targets. It made a sound that made everyone cringe.

"Good night," I said as I swung my sword to slice his head off. His body disintegrated in the air and I looked back and saw the rest of the people rush me. I stabbed them one by one until there was nobody standing but me.

I saw the clock and noticed it had taken me a full six minutes — I was getting rusty. I gave out a very creepy grin and threw my sword straight behind me. I did not hear my blade hit the floor for a good twenty seconds.

As I turned around, I saw a man standing with a knife falling from his hands, as my blade stuck in his chest over his heart. I walked over to the guy and removed my sword from his chest. I turned around and saw the platform getting farther and farther away from me.

I started to run after it but obstacles started to get in my way. I managed to dodge all the obstacles but now the platform was gaining altitude. I looked at how much time I had and the clock countdown read 00:13:34:56. *What was happening?*

More and more obstacles impeded my progress. Suddenly, a light bulb went off in my head. I started to use the obstacles to my advantage as I catapulted myself from one pillar to the next as I gained speed and height to close the distance on the platform.

But then, the pillars stopped appearing and I only had twenty seconds left on the clock before I failed the mission. I did what first came to mind. I jumped from my current pillar to the platform, but I was off by around three inches.

I grabbed my sword and stabbed Justification into the platform. I struggled to pull myself onto the platform and chided myself that the rust in my bones was real.

I looked around at the platform and saw a guy who applauded me and said, "Great job!"

I walked over to the man who handed me a folder with all the details on the targeted teacher. The folder told me everything I needed to know, including his age, address, background, and a list of the corrupt things he had done. He was a monster! I left the organization building and headed back to my house to pack my bags.

I packed everything into my car and drove about three hours to a beautiful, small valley called Arroyo Grande. I was amazed such a gorgeous place could support such a horrid man as the teacher.

I had told the organization that I did not need lodging because I planned to finish the mission in less than a day, but they insisted I stay and infiltrate the school, posing as a transfer student. I found the hotel they had booked for me and was impressed by its charm.

I relaxed in my comfy bed and looked over the folder of the target whose name was Rafael Varela. He had been teaching for over seven years but had become dirty about two years ago when he began smuggling money, drugs, and technology from foreign places. My objective was to find his stash and assassinate Mr. Varela. Should be easy enough.

The next morning, I made my way to his school classroom at the Arroyo Grande High School in classroom 44B. My first instinct was to look around the school for that stash. I cautiously entered a long, empty hallway, which I found oddly quiet and empty.

All of the sudden, I heard the footsteps of a woman in high heels walking behind me. I anticipated finding a teacher, and turned around with the plan to lie and ask for direction. But before I could turn, I heard her voice.

It was so soothing and relaxing. It was unreal and a tear strangely fell from my eye. Before I could say or do anything, she was gone. I looked everywhere but I could not see anyone.

I started to tap my head with my fist very softly as I tried to remember what she had said.

What had she said?

What are you doing here? *Was that it?*

You shouldn't be here. *Was that it?*

I thought that I must be dreaming and that I needed to refocus on my mission. I did not see anywhere that it looked possible for Mr. Varela to stash anything. I remembered my cover as a transfer student and quickly went to the class listed on my schedule provided by the organization. I was not worried because I had been tutored for years and was adept at nearly all the subjects.

After the day at school, I went back to my hotel. But all I could think about was the woman's voice I had heard.

If only I had turned around faster when I heard her voice, I would be certain it was her.

As I arrived at my hotel, the atmosphere felt weird. Suddenly, I felt a presence behind me. I could see that it was a man through the reflection in a window located north from me. He was holding a blade with a familiar symbol on it and was wearing a holster on his left hip that was similar to mine.

I pretended like I did not see him and just nonchalantly went down to the hotel basement area. I sped up so I could lose the man behind me. I hid behind a small pillar and climbed into a small hole in the attic to wait to attack the man. As he passed beneath me, I hopped down and grabbed his startled form.

"Why are you following me?" I asked impatiently.

"I just came down here to catch some clean air and take a stroll," the man smirked.

"You have approximately ten seconds to tell me who sent you or I will kill you five," I smirked in return as I pushed him in front of me so I could get a good look at him.

"Da-yaam, so scary. I'm just here to make new friends," he said with a little frown.

"Time's up," I said with finality.

I reached over my shoulder as if I was stretching. I grasped my blade but did not withdraw it from the holster so it would not become visible to the human eye. He withdrew his sword and assumed a simple swordsman pose. I honestly felt sorry for the fellow. I withdrew my sword from its holster and held it in front of me.

As I prepared for this real world kill, I repeated the mantra, "Light as a feather and ready to kill."

I took a deep breath, opened my eyes, and said, "Good night, may your rest last for eternity."

As I rapidly ran towards him, the rings around my pupils became crimson red as if a demon had possessed me. My sword has sliced straight through his right hand as blood splattered all over the floor.

"You have less than three seconds to tell me who sent you before you bleed out," I asked nicely.

He remained quiet and died quickly.

I looked through his clothes for any information on who had put the mark on me. I found a little paper that had an address — clearly this was an important place. Since I was tired, I decided to go to my room and sleep the night away and figure out what to do over the weekend.

On that Saturday, I decided to go to the address and see what was there. When I arrived after the long drive, there was a big building with a lot of people in suits. Among the people, I spotted Mr. Varela talking to a man with a small, but bushy beard whose hair seemed to have grayed from stress.

I discreetly followed them as went into a room that looked empty. But when they closed the door, I could hear a lot of activity coming from inside. I also overheard them talking about where the secret stash was.

Very convenient.

I had a lot of thoughts in my mind as I started to leave. The weekend went by very quickly since I just stayed in my hotel to avoid any unnecessary interactions. On Monday, I went to the hiding place in the back of the school library where they had said the stash was, carefully looking around for trip wires. Finding none, I left most of the stuff in the safe place and quickly grabbed a few hundred dollar bills and forms of technology that I had never seen in my life. But I didn't see drugs anywhere. I cleaned all my fingerprints and left a micro camera behind to see who went back to the stash hiding place.

Later that week, while I was in my AP Calculus class, I looked at my camera through my phone and noticed there was a familiar woman's shape at the stash.

No, it couldn't be.

I asked my teacher if I could be excused because I wasn't feeling well. I rushed over to the stash and I saw Abby.

My heart started to beat faster as I saw her reach into the stash. Suddenly, I noticed she had a sword on her back; it was identical to mine. I reached over my shoulder to see if Justification was still there.

My trusty weapon remained available but invisible to the untrained human eye.

I was in shock and all I could think was to get her out of that room. I ran over to the closest security guard and informed him that there was a student ditching class in the secret room. The guard ran over to the room and went in to check it out. A few moments later, I saw the guard escorting Abby out of the room.

Abby saw me, looked down, and continued to walk by me. The look on her eyes saddened and confused me because she looked disappointed for some reason. In a way, I felt like the sentiment was not directed at me but at herself. As I walked over to the main entrance, I saw her outside the principal's office waiting for someone. I remained quiet and continued walking past her.

As I passed by her, I heard her mumble, "I'm sorry."

I continued as if I did not hear her. I found a big bag to store all the cash. I went back to the school and snuck into the secret stash room and started putting everything in the big bag.

I felt a presence looking at me, but when I turned around there was nobody in sight. Then, a whispered question sent chills up my spine.

"Why couldn't you have told me?" asked a very faint voice.

At that moment, I knew Abby was in the room spying on me. I got the bag but kept cool like I still thought I was alone. I left like I did not hear her and then pretended to swiftly go to my car. But it was all a ruse as I ducked behind a large pillar to let her pass me. Just as she passed, I grabbed her by her sword's holster.

"I knew you missed me, but I didn't realize it was enough for you to follow me all this way," I said as I held her holster in one hand and combed back my hair with my other hand.

"How are you so good at knowing where I'm at and how did you see my blade?" she asked me with teary eyes, that were on the brink of spilling over.

I looked her dead in the eyes and pointed to the sacred symbol on the sword and said, "Answer me this. Where did you get this blade?

It's from a secret series of swords that only specially trained people can use."

Abby's eyes narrowed as she responded, "How do you know so much of the series? It's not like you have one of these, since there are only three in existence."

"Just answer the question, please," I insisted

"It was given to me by an old, wise man when I was a child training in the A.O.C.," she replied quietly as she knowingly referred to the Assassination Organization Corporation by its acronym.

My eyes widened, as I was rendered speechless. So many memories went through my head. Many of those memories were of my own childhood growing up in the A.O.C. where I was haunted by an enemy whom I could never exactly distinguish. The closest I ever got to glimpsing a real visual was only of a person with short hair, whom I had assumed to be a boy. Over time, my battles with my enemy lessened and by the time I was ten, I no longer engaged with my rival. And, at age eleven, the blade Justification was bestowed upon me.

As I looked deeply into Abby's eyes, I asked her if she remembered having a rival in the A.O.C. She remained quiet and just broke out of my hold. She asked for her sword back and stormed away. I tried following her, but I could tell from her tense body language that she was furious with what the world had done to her and there was no way that we could speak honestly to each other at that time.

As I left the school area, I quickly realized that several assassins must have arrived in town and they all seemed to be thirsty for my head. I did not want to draw my sword because there were too many cameras, which would have recorded my secretly trained skills for the whole world. Darkness had fallen just as my enemies were realizing the extent of my skills, as they fell to the ground in contorted messes. I returned my sword to its sheath as I surveyed the thirty assassins who painted the ground with their crimson blood.

From behind me, a very faint voice called me over. Before I could even make out what words were being said, I realized my feet were walking towards the voice's direction. I stared at my own feet in consternation as I realized I had no control over my own body that was moving towards the voice. As I got nearer the shadowy figure, my eyes clamped shut — I could not open them no matter what will power I summoned. Suddenly, I felt a breath caressing the back of my neck and then the unmistakable sensation of a gentle kiss…

I instantly knew it was Abby, so I tried my very best to break out of her enchantment that had taken control of my movements.

When I broke out of the spell, I grabbed her, gave her a huge hug, and said, "Why did you have to leave me? You could have told me that you were in the A.O.C."

A tear fell from her left eye, and then another fell from her right one as she replied, "I'm an assassin. I kill people for a living and a holder of Karitasu."

I hugged her tighter and whispered, "What does you being a holder of Karitasu… What does that have to do with anything?"

Her tears stopped and silence pervaded the space around us.

She continued in a solemn tone, "Listen up. People want me dead. One of whom is a holder of a sword from the Kari series."

"I know for a fact that the holder of Justification is not the one trying to kill you. So, it must be the holder of Karidisu. Do you know who wields Karidisu?"

Abby's eyes flashed at me in unexpected anger and she yelled, "How do you know who wields Justification?"

She pushed me away from her and shouted, "The wielder of Karidisu is dead. I killed him."

Although I was worried for her safety, I kept calm and asked her, "Do you have the blade of Karidisu?"

"No! I'm an assassin, not a thief," she replied with indignation. "So, the one that wants me dead is the one with Justification."

I knew things were coming to a head, so I took a step back, reached over my shoulder, and grabbed my blade. As I started to remove the blade, she adopted a battle stance.

"Do you know what this blade can do?" I asked, with the sword fully drawn. "This is the demon's blade. It can make the wielder become a demon that can send all the low-life scum humans to hell."

I could see that Abby was shaking with nerves as her sword shook in her trembling hands.

I continued and said, "I will not be using this blade on you, Abby. But I will be using this blade today."

I could see that a huge weight had been lifted from her shoulders as relief flowed through her body.

A sarcastic, loud clapping sound broke the silence as I registered the figure of the man who had given me the job. He steadily approached as my eyes focused in on his every move.

"Why must you ruin everything Agent A?" he sputtered with anger. "I should have known that I could not fool you. After all, I taught you everything you know"

Abby stepped behind me as she held her karitasu ready to battle this enemy.

The man nodded to Abby, "And you why aren't you happy to see me? The last time you saw me was when you stabbed me and killed me. Ha! I bet you're surprised."

Abby was mumbling words of anger under her breath as she stepped out from behind me to flank the enemy opposite to my position.

I, too, was mumbling, but not just the words of the anger I felt, but the words of enchantment, "Scum who brings misfortune to humankind will be brought down to the depths of hell. The wrath of Lucifer will bring you to justice."

My whole eyes had become black.

"Abby, you with me on this?" I asked my new ally in this epic battle.

Her whole eyes had become blood red.

She nodded her head and we both charged the man from different directions.

At this moment, I awoke from the dream.

Even as an old man, I wanted a dream like that to happen in this world.

17

Vector to the Heavens

By

Damien Donato

Chapter 1: Joining the Rebellion

I used to do a lot in my spare time before the king changed it all

and left us in a "brighter future" that seemed dimmer than the past

ever was. It was no longer a country like in the olden days where

bells tolled or children played. It was more like a totalitarian

wasteland where the new king and his police made life a living hell.

The police were not like the police of olden days either. The new

police were more like guards who terrorized people.

But today seemed to be kind of an odd day. There were no police

roaming the city streets of Caliber or any sign of them anywhere. In

my daily routine of working in the king's courtyard, I noticed that the king was not outside standing on his granite-carved balcony watching

his peasants.

Where is he? Is he taking a day off from pushing people around?

I took my mind off it and went back to clearing the courtyard of

weeds.

I went back to my dwelling and asked my fellow citizen, "Has

the king made an announcement about his absence?"

They said that they had not heard anything. Everyone was unsure

of what was happening. I went inside my dwelling filled with simple,

wood-carved furniture, which I learned to make in my spare time. I

headed to a stairwell and followed the stairs to a door marked

"Fallout Shelter" and sat inside to read my secretly pilfered books.

I had no idea what a "fallout" was, but I could sound out words

and match them to sounds I say and hear. I had covertly collected

any books left behind in the king's courtyard.

Reading them gave me color in this gray world that was ruled

with a heavy hand.

I read books about hope and friendship, good and evil, and love and hate.

Reading these books could get me executed, but in truth, the tantalizing thoughts of hope and freedom were probably a punishment worse than death. Learning wise words from Gandhi's speeches or John Locke's "right to rebel and civil disobedience" fueled a desire for rebellion. I fell asleep later that cold night to dreams of how I could better that world.

Weird visions interrupted my slumber — like screeching premonitions of a dead society that someone had created. I awoke screaming and shocked from this dream that left me to wonder: *was it I, or was it someone else?*

I shook off the dream's unpleasant memories and headed back to my regular room where I dressed in some torn brown pants and a black shirt that was a bit too big. I left my house to find the air was unbearably hot and humid, the streets empty, and the window shutters closed. I guessed that a storm was coming and that everyone was inside to avoid the rain. I strolled along the trail of dirt that led to the king's palace.

I stopped dead in my tracks — a dead body lay in the middle of the street.

Did the person collapse from the heat?

I bent to check the body for signs of life and was immediately drawn in by a mysterious silver pennant the old man had around his neck. I was amazed by its design that showed two swords melded together like a cross. I was startled as the old man gasped and grabbed my shirt collar.

"The vector…. the vector is alive," he whispered in my ear.

"Vector? What Vector?" I asked him.

"The key to…. a better… future…" he managed to say with his last breath.

I disentangled myself from his grip as stared at him in wonder. I realized that this pennant must mean something bigger than just the two of us.

I hurried away before anyone noticed me and returned to my dwelling. I locked the door behind me, shuttered my own windows, and started looking through all of my secret books for any information. Just as I found a link connecting the symbol to a group from the year 3019, a knock at the door shook me out of my research.

"Evan, open up. I need a word with you," called the king to me from the other side of the door.

This was strange. What did he want with a lowly courtyard cleaner?

I opened the door to see the normally regal king dressed in modern clothes.

"Come in, my king," I said as I ushered him into my humble home.

"Evan, my boy. I saw you from my balcony and you were talking to that dying old fool. What did he tell you?" the king asked me point blank.

Nervous, I choked a bit and cleared my throat, "Well, my lord Pagan, he was just asking for water. But I didn't care. He was already dying. Why bother?"

The king looked me dead in the eye.

Does he know I'm lying? This man could order me killed me in a split second or order me tortured without end.

The king seemed somewhat satisfied and said, "Well, my boy. I best be returning to my royal duties. Stay safe since you know…. a storm is coming."

"Sure thing, your majesty. Long live the king."

As he exited the door, he turned to me and I could not help but notice an ominous smirk on his face.

I sat on my chair with my heart still pounding hard and sweat pouring out of my skin like there was no tomorrow. I pushed myself up off the chair and went to the water pump. I drank a full glass of cool water as I collected my thoughts.

Was that old man a rebel? Was there a rebellion brewing? Did the king's guards kill the old man? Why did they leave the old man in the street? What was the meaning of the silver pennant?

So many questions swirled in my mind that I had to sleep to calm my mind.

A loud bang woke me from my nightmares and I quickly went downstairs. I saw three masked figures around the same height as me in my entryway. I was paralyzed with fear as they took off their masks to reveal their faces. A woman and two well-built men looked at me and I saw the same silver pennant on their attire.

"Are you part of the resistance?" I blurted out.

They nodded and one of the men said, "That snake Pagan is coming for you. Come with us to the vector."

Without hesitation, I packed some of my belongings in a torn bag that had the words "M.S.A." on it and swiftly disembarked with the rebels. I glanced back at my home and, suddenly, a huge explosion engulfed my dwelling in flames. I realized Pagan thought I was part of this group and had tried to mercilessly assassinate me.

And I started to consider returning the favor.

Chapter 2: Ways of a Warrior

I went with the rebels and asked questions about the resurrection of the rebel force.

"We were just fed up with their bull," one of the rebels said.

"Yeah, Pagan thought the group was extinguished, but we kept everything in operation right under his nose. But then he caught wind of our operations and our comrades went missing one by one," added the masked woman.

Everything started to make sense as I said, "So, that's why streets were vacant this morning?"

The masked man replied, "We don't know exactly why the streets were so empty this morning. But over the past few weeks, our reports have revealed that the king was conducting a genocide and picking them off one by one, killing more and more."

I was shocked that all this had been happening while I was just clearing weeds from the courtyard.

After I gained the trust of the rebels, I asked them their names, which were revealed as Xion, Mason, and Ven. We set out on a journey to another village located in the southwest wasteland of Bunker Hill.

As dawn approached, I passed through the village gates made from solid metal that was being heated by the sun's rays and were already hot to the touch. A big sign read "Welcome home." It seemed like a beautiful place where life sprang from the earth and the fields were filled with joyous children playing and laughing.

As I walked through the city, I noticed that the buildings were made of salvaged metal and wood, which fortified it against attack. In the wasteland, there was nothing but sand and ruins as it was plagued by radiation storms from the south that blew from the northeast.

"Evan, over here," Xion called.

I walked casually towards a large tent filled with handmade rifles. The weapons were a bit crude but were made from metal forged carefully together by a skilled craftsman.

"This is our headquarters. It's not much, but it's something," Venn said

"I thought you guys had more people than just you three," I said in surprise.

"I wouldn't say that," a man of high stature with an old scar across his face said. His voice and presence caught me off guard as I turned to greet this new rebel.

"I'm the ringleader of this rowdy organization. There are about 20 of us, but we can sure pack a hell of a punch," he said with ferocity.

I chuckled at this battle-wise giant who added, "Name's Robert. My spies managed to take you out of that hellhole faster than I thought," he said.

"Yeah, they saved my life," I smiled.

"Evan, welcome to the warriors. I know it's a crappy name, but it's good enough," Robert said with a laugh.

The other rebels laughed at this statement, which was obviously a running joke in their rebel camp.

Robert said to me, "Mason will get you up to speed on some details on our next operation. He's by the big tree just at the edge of the settlement. Xion will walk down with you."

I nodded and went to the tree that looked like it been growing there before the bombs fell. It had grown from a healthy seed before the radiation had polluted everything. I had only read about fruit growing from a tree but had never seen it happening in real life.

"Beautiful isn't it," Mason pulled me from my thoughts on the growing fruit.

He took out a half-smoked cigarette, relit it, and took a smooth puff as he eyed me up and down. Xion panned the horizon with her hand shielding her eyes from the sun.

"Rob sent you over to me to learn about the mission, right?" he asked.

I nodded.

"You need to learn how to shoot to kill because we are gonna take the fight to Pagan," he sternly said.

I looked at the side of the tree to notice a rusty pipe rifle that must be what was used for target practice. I wondered how many newbie rebels had practiced on the can.

Mason noticed where my eyes were looking and said, "Just pick it up."

I picked up the makeshift pipe rifle, aimed it towards a can riddled with bullet holes, and squeezed the trigger.

"Nice shot," Mason said.

Xion quickly added, "We got to teach you more than to shoot."

Chapter 3: The Fight

My days became filled with learning battle and survival skills.

Robert took me under his wing and praised every lesson I mastered.

"Good, Evan! You're getting the hang of this!" Robert said after I managed to scramble to the top of a cliff and shoot a feral dog from about 125 yards away with a modified rifle.

This was it. Robert called me down to join in the last supper before we embarked on our raid on the king's castle. I jumped down from the 15-foot cliff and nearly landed on my face. I still had a lot of skills to learn, but my ego was soothed when Robert said that I was one of the best shots in the group.

The stars shown like pristine diamonds in the sheltering sky, which masked the horror that we were about to discover.

The settlement was a scorched mess of flames and dead comrades. Pagan's royal guards were attacking the camp! One spotted me and rushed towards me. I grabbed my serrated combat knife and sliced his throat. I threw his bleeding body to the ground and raced over to the arsenal to find a rifle. I snatched one in my hands and started shooting at the enemy invaders.

"Take these bastards down!" shouted Robert as he motioned my attention to a guard leader who was loading a missile launcher. I had to stop him from firing that missile that would decimate our forces. I concentrated through all the commotion and shot him square in the chest. But to no avail. He had on body armor! He was a leader of the guards!

I could see Rob searching through the wounded trying to give them medical attention. I continued trying to take down the leader as I fired round after round that did no damage. Finally, his helmet came off in the fray. As he was distractedly trying to refasten his helmet, I rushed forward for a better position and shot his right between the eyes.

I knew that bastard was dead, but adrenaline pulsed through my veins and I savagely took my knife and cut off his head. With my face splattered with my prey's blood, I held up the guard leader's head high in the air for all to see. This was my vengeance on behalf of all those who could not protect themselves from Pagan's merciless guards.

"ROB!!" I yelled out.

"I'm right here, Evan!"

I ran through the fires and flames to Rob's side.

"Where are Ven, Mason, or Xion, Rob?" I asked nervously.

"They're right there," Rob pointed to the trio who were attending to those injured in this atrocity.

I shouted to them over the loud noises, "What about the mission?"

"We have to abandon that plan! There are too many injured. There's no way we can pull it off," Xion said as she pressed the bleeding wounds of an injured soldier.

In the heat of frustration and anger, I snapped, "I don't need you guys. I can go kill that asshole myself."

The others were shocked by my decision as I grabbed some gear for my personal mission. I left in the next fifteen minutes, not knowing the fate of my comrades or if I would ever return to this "home" again.

Chapter 4: Vengeance

I half-ran, half-walked to the Castle and was out of breath by the time I reached its foreboding edifice. I stealthily approached the walls and wondered if it would be easy to sneak in because so many guards were away or if there would be lots of booby traps to watch out for.

Suddenly, I felt a presence following close behind me. I guessed that the fight would be starting before I even entered the city walls. I clutched my knife and whirled around to kill my enemy.

Thank God for my quick reflexes because I was just able to stop myself from killing my comrade Xion. She had followed me the whole way but had been too far behind to catch up to me until then.

"You can't do this by yourself," she whispered.

"I know I can't, but it feels nice that I now probably won't die alone," I said with a chuckle that made her laugh as well.

We plotted our attack by going through the tunnels, which we thought might not have as many traps as other entryways. We made our way through the dark, rank tunnels and found a street cover hole where we could ascend to the courtyard. When we got to the surface, we quickly realized that the whole place was a minefield — literally.

We helped each other tiptoe across the minefield as we balanced step-by-step until a sneaky little mouse ran across a mine and blew the whole courtyard sky high. Luckily, Xion and I were close enough to safety and just suffered a few bruises.

"Sh*t!!!" I exclaimed and a few royal guards came out from the main door with weapons ready to kill. One of them came near us as we hid behind a wall. He came closer and I held my knife ready to end his life smoothly and quickly. But I decided against the blood spilling on the floor and arousing suspicion. So, I snuck up behind him and broke his neck. Xion grabbed his gun and I took his armor as we made it inside the castle without detection. We continued up the marble steps and managed to make it to Pagan's room. But when we opened the door, we found another commander waiting for us with a combat shotgun. One bullet flew into my shoulder sending me flying across the floor. Luckily, Xion kept her wits about her and put two bullets in his head.

"Get up, lazy butt," Xion said to me with a smile.

"I just got shot," I wheezed.

"But you're alive," she said in a tone that made me smile as well.

But all the dark humor would have to wait as I heard footsteps coming from the stairs. I found a bag of explosives behind the dead commander's feet. I placed and scattered them around the four corners of the room. Xion and I ran to the building's top floor — I was sure that that was where Pagan was hiding.

Xion and I pushed open the top floor door only to be met with an army of men standing with guns, all trained on us.

The only word I could say was…. "Damn."

Chapter 5: The Future That Won't Live to Be

Pagan emerged from behind his small army and said, "Evan, you have some balls storming in here. That is some sh*t I might even respect. But you failed this time boy!"

Xion and I looked to each other and broke into a run with our guns blazing. Another bullet knocked me back down a flight of stairs.

Xion turned to me and shouted, "Evan, get up!"

Without a thought, I took several of the grenades I had taken out of the bag of explosives. I pulled out the pins and threw them each in perfect arcs over Xion's head and into the enemy space.

After the explosions, I heard shouts of agony as blood started flowing down the steps. I struggled back up the steps to try to find Xion, but I knew she had sacrificed herself for our cause. Mangled body parts littered the castle room and I saw the final moments of Pagan's wretched life as he groped at his eyeball that was dangling from his eye socket. He only had the one arm still attached to his body.

Exhausted, I slumped on the ground in the pool of violence that I had been a part of. I thought back over all the battle lessons I had received from Robert, Mason, and the others. And I thought about the old man whose dying words and whose silver pennant had instigated this whole coup. I had just been a lowly courtyard gardener who had a secret stash of books, but now I had become a world-weary rebel who had left his sanity in the violence of battle.

18

The Man in the Black Hood

By

Roy Vasquez

Got to keep moving. Got to keep moving.

Was I swimming or was I walking? Where was I?

My body just kept moving and the waves kept slapping my face and the branches kept scratching my face.

I was on my stomach and the sand was crawling into my mouth and it was pitch black. I rolled over onto my back as the bright sun stabbed my memory awake.

Plane crash — Mayday! Mayday!

Now, I was the king of nowhere, of a little island with no one to rule over and no one to save me, except myself.

I saw the beast moving through the forest.

I hunched in the bushes and covered myself with more mud.

Was I going to kill this animal and eat it and survive?

And then would I find another animal, kill it, eat it, and survive?

Augh!!!!

The jaguar lunged out of the bushes and grew into the shape of a full-grown man who plunged a sword into my chest.

***

The scent of dank water and waxy candles infiltrated my nose as the lights flickered against the glistening cave walls.

I cautiously parted my eyes a sliver to see swords, bows, and axes all stacked against the cave walls. On a rock near the arsenal, there sat the cloaked figure of the jaguar-human wearing a black hood that obscured his entire face.

"Who are you?" he growled at me.

"My name is Roy Vasquez and I'm from Los Angeles, California," I stammered. "I mean no harm. I'm rich and can give you whatever you want if you help me get back home."

The man in the black hood sighed and threw more twigs on the small fire that warmed the dank cave.

"There is no way home. You're the first person I've seen for the past decade," he said with resignation.

A decade? My mind reeled as I slumped back into unconsciousness.

I felt a cool rag being swathed across my forehead and his voice telling me of how he found me and brought me to the cave. His reassuring voice carried me into a deep slumber.

Every day became a training ground where the man in the black hood taught me how to survive by hunting with crude bows and arrows and swords and knives. I learned how to be a stealthy, silent jaguar myself as I stalked unwitting prey.

He taught me lesson after lesson and skill after skill; but he never removed his black hood. I never asked him to remove it, though sometimes I knew he could sense that my curiosity was burning in my mind and heart.

We passed an eternity on the small island as hurricanes ripped whole coconut trees from the earth and we hunkered down in the safety of our cave. I became a skilled hunter and could shoot one arrow through two parrots in one pluck of my bow.

But beyond eating, my hunting and killing skills never had true meaning until the fateful day when the man in the black hood stopped moving and laid in the cave for his last breaths. I held my mentor in my arms as I gazed down at the mouth of the hooded face where the fabric of the hood went in and out with each of the man's last struggling breaths.

The fire danced across the cave walls and a sense of parting and sorrow started to fill me as I began to grieve for the imminent passing of my mentor and my imminent loneliness.

"Disciple, son, take off the hood," I heard the hooded voice whisper.

I reached under the back of the hood and carefully held the back of my mentor's neck. I pulled the hood over my teacher's head and saw the face beneath the mask — it was a woman's face.

I gasped in shock as she gasped for air.

Over the years, we had developed an unspoken bond that bordered on telepathy. But I did not imagine this.

Everything became clear as she silently pressed a small book into my hands. I opened it to see that it held a list of names.

The woman who had worn the black hood gathered her last strength and said, "These are the cursed names of the cursed people who marooned me on the island."

She had never said how she had arrived on the island or told me anything about her past. I had just accepted the past as the past and that the present had been about learning survival skills. But now, I realized that all those times I entrapped a boar or had speared a shark, she had been envisioning me as entrapping and spearing her enemies.

This person in the black hood was my mentor and I would honor her and avenge the wrongs committed against her.

I buried my mentor and washed out the black hood in the bitterness of the salty sea as I strengthened my resolve to escape from this deserted paradise to fulfill my destiny.

With the black hood now firmly over my head and face, I sat in meditation as I pondered how I would finally get off this cursed island. I had been so wrapped up in learning the art of survival from my mentor that I had almost lost thought of returning to society. I had come to think of civilization as just a rat race where people worked hard just to pay for fancy things. It had all come to be so fake and fruitless.

But now I had a mission. My mentor needed her vengeance and I was the vehicle of retribution.

I had explored nearly every inch of the island except for the foreboding cliff of death on the eastern side. The cliffs were above a bay that had calm, clear waters. I could use the serene waters to take a raft out past the breakers. Only problem was what was visible beneath those clear waters — sharks.

Yes, my only way off the island's circle of intense waves was through an estuary for baby sharks. Babies or not, they still had teeth.

I climbed the cliff and peered into the waters. The sharks were two and three feet long and swarmed and fought with each other for each unfortunate morsel of food they could find. These shark pups were no puppies and they were ready for their first real taste of blood.

I lay on the edge of the cliff and looked over it. So, I would need to build a raft and a rope made of leaves in order to climb down this terrifying cliff. There was no other safe way to get into the shark-infested water that would lead me to the open waters.

I pushed myself up to a standing position and scanned the horizon that held my future and my fate. My mind burned with the desire to avenge my mentor and I turned back into the jungle to begin building my raft and rope.

I ripped hundreds of branches and leaves from the trees and used my legs to break and kick down trunks of bamboo trees to build a raft. By firelight at night, I wove the large leaves into a rope and wove the bamboo logs into a solid raft. I had made rafts before, but this one would need to withstand the open ocean.

I made it twice as big as any raft I had made before. Halfway through, I had to transition to working on it outside the cave because it had grown too large. My fingers were swollen and bleeding as I finished the last of the feet of the rope and affixed the last of the bamboo slates for the raft.

Exhausted, I sat staring into the fire praying for a ship to pass by and pick me up. I could hear the weather picking up and the wind was growing stronger by the day. I would need to leave as the low-tide water was drawing into the ocean. I thought about all those shark pups that could easily attack my raft then sharpened a few more bamboo spears for good measure. Besides, who knew what I would encounter in the vast ocean?

I dragged my raft to the shores of the ocean and pushed off. I floated into the dark sea for countless hours, drifting in and out of sleep. Suddeny, I saw the blinding lights of a cruise ship. I survived.

When I made it back home, everything looked so different. I saw new buildings and new people in a world where I needed to reconnect with old friends and family. As I passed by newspaper stands and glanced at the horrifying headlines, I knew that it was also a world that had grown more violent.

Through the busy streets, I finally made it to my house. After three years, it was exactly as I remembered it as I reached for the familiar doorknob. When I finally saw my mom, I hugged her as hard as I had ever hugged anyone.

My mom cried and said, "I knew you weren't dead. I knew everyone was wrong."

Then, she took me to my room where I saw my long-forgotten bed that called to me like an old friend. I rushed to my bed and jumped on it with a sudden, childish glee. It was one of the best feelings ever. I saw old pictures of my family and when I looked at the old pictures of myself, I saw how young and innocent I had been. Now, I knew the ways of the world and I had a mission. No more jumping on the bed for me — I was a man who needed to avenge his master. And I knew I would need to protect my identity and plans in order to achieve this goal.

The next day, I went off to look for Cynthia. I was hoping she did not have anyone new in her life. I wanted to win her heart again and start a life with her like we once had. Instead, I received terrible news. Everyone I asked said that they had not heard from her in over a week. I felt shocked and surprised.

Immediately, I began searching for her. I searched for days in the light of day, but I found nothing. It was time I looked for her in the night. I donned my master's black hoodie and grabbed my bow and quiver. Under this disguise, I searched for Cynthia.

As I walked the streets, the noises of violence filled the air — sirens, shouting, screaming, crying. Suddenly, the crying was coming from the alley I was just passing. I stopped and peered at the two struggling forms in the darkness.

I realized what was happening — a gangster was trying to kidnap and rape a girl.

Not on my watch!

I jumped up in the gangster's face and pried the girl out of his arms. She ran to the alley wall and struggled to catch her breath. I stepped back to get a clear look and shot at this ruffian.

He looked at me in shock, "Who do you think you are?"

"They call me the Dark Archer," I said with a steady voice as I shot an arrow into his shoulder.

He pulled out a gun and shot back at me. I dodged the bullets and lunged forward to grab his arm. With my other hand, I grabbed the arrow in his shoulder and twisted it further in.

He yelped like a scared little puppy.

I did not show any mercy and I interrogated him, "Where were you gonna take the girl? Where?"

His voice trembled as he answered, "To a building south from here. Now, let me go, you freak!"

I knocked him out as I saw the terrified girl run across the street to the safety of her apartment.

I made my way to the building the gangster had described. I was surprised, but I was nervous. I was not afraid of battling whatever I might find there. I realized that I was afraid of finding Cynthia in such a terrible place. I steeled my courage and prepared myself for whatever I might find in the building. I was a protector and it was my duty to free any kidnapped women and to bring hope to this destitute city.

When I got to the neighborhood, I silently climbed up the fire escape of an abandoned building in order to search for the building that seemed to be a hiding place for these low life gangsters. I went from rooftop to rooftop searching for the exact building and finally found it.

I noticed one specific building amongst all the burnt out abandoned ones, that was jacked up with cameras. Gangsters seemed to be constantly going in and out. I knew I had to free the girls, even if I was outnumbered.

I peered into the building itself through a broken window. I started the battle off with taking out two gangsters with one arrow. I jumped into the building and landed on a walkway high above the gangsters. It was like shooting fish in a barrel. I easily shot most of them with my arrows. Only five of those jokers remained and I jumped right in the middle of all five. They came toward me, and one of them managed to stab my leg. I kept shooting arrows even though I was bleeding. I took down the rest of those fools and busted open the door where the women were being held prisoner.

They were free at last.

I searched the freed women for my precious Cynthia, but none of them had heard or seen her. I was worried but kept searching. Terrible thoughts darted around in my mind.

Is she dead?

If she's dead, did she suffer?

All the freed women ran to the door and into the streets to find their ways to the police station to file reports. For myself, I realized that I did not want to be a part of the police reports and that I had to clean my blood from the building floor. I did not want the police to trace me.

Even though the men had been criminals, I had committed murder. I was no longer just another citizen, but the Dark Archer. As I dragged the dead men over my bloodstain in order to hide my DNA, I realized that even if I found Cynthia, she might not accept me as the new person I had become. I wasn't the same person she had known and she might fear my new calling as a crime crusader.

The next day, I went to an abandoned factory my father used to own. I set up a secret base where I could hide and spy on the city. I hacked into the city's CCTV systems and the police scanners in order to watch and listen to every move made in this dark city. I made this base my home where I practiced my archery and searched the city for my beloved Cynthia.

"Car 52, please respond to situation with a blonde woman dressed in black who is wearing a mask. Bystanders are saying that she's carrying a staff that seems to be able to be separated into two. Proceed with caution," the dispatcher announced.

My ears perked up. I knew it was not Cynthia because she was not blonde and did not know how to fight with a staff; but this situation caught my attention

I followed the Dispatcher's directions and went down to the glades to find this mysterious woman. I beat the cops there and snuck up behind her.

"Who are you?" I asked her.

"*Alkunria al'Aswad*," she responded.

My heart skipped a beat since I knew that that meant "Black Canary" in Arabic. I looked into her eyes and noticed something familiar.

No, it could not be.

I stepped back in shock and shouted, "No!"

She threw a dagger directly into my shoulder. I cried out in surprise, but steeled my strength since I had been stabbed on several occasions on the island.

I retreated to fight another day. The Black Canary was truly a formidable foe and I needed to protect the city from her dangerous designs. But I needed help.

I had wanted to do this on my own, but I knew that I needed to draw on my family resources from Vasquez Consolidated to conquer this enemy. Back at my secret base, I cleansed my wound and dressed it. I also planned my next move. My mother had taken the company reigns after my father's death. Being a modern woman, she had gathered some of the best IT minds on the planet. This included

Emily Brett, who was the skilled hacker I knew.

I just hoped that I could convince her to join my crusade. I

searched my databases to find her home, where I went to secretly

meet with her. I broke into her empty house and rifled through her

papers and things. I found copious notes that seemed to be

researching the last hours of her husband's day a few weeks prior.

Her husband, Christopher Brett, was a lawyer. So, I immediately

knew that gangsters had taken him.

Maybe this is a way to help her and get her to join my cause?

I decided to find out what I could about a link between Cynthia

and Christopher's kidnapping. Both were taken on the same day, but

at different times. So, the people who took Christopher could be the

same ones who took Cynthia.

I approached Emily with this information and she responded with

tears in her eyes that she would do anything to get her husband back

safe and sound.

I asked her to hack Christopher's office security system to find the footage of the night he was kidnapped.

I was shocked to see the Black Canary shoving the startled Christopher into a van. The urge to find Cynthia grew stronger.

"Emily, I want you to hack into all the city's security cameras and find where the Black Canary was last seen."

She ran a complex hacker program of her own design, which isolated people's figures and general clothing.

"Ah!" Emily shouted in shock. "She was last seen at Vasquez Consolidated."

Emily turned her chair around to face me. I fell into complete silence, but then I mustered my strength and grabbed my bow.

"Try to capture her, but if you can't — put this tracker on her shoe," Emily said as she handed me a dime-size tracking device.

As I made for the door, I called over my shoulder, "Emily, be my other set of eyes."

I knew I could trust her and that she was just as invested in this mission as I was.

When I entered my family's company headquarters, I saw broken glass everywhere.

I whispered to Emily, "Where's the Black Canary now?"

Emily replied, "She's in your office."

I stealthily ran towards my old office where I found the deadly Black Canary nonchalantly staring at a picture of my family.

I was enraged and shouted, "Put that down!"

I had already drawn an arrow and I narrowed my focus in for the kill.

"In 2015, you took Christopher Brett and Cynthia Garcia. Where are they! I'll put an arrow in you if you don't tell me!"

This witch started weaving a tale to prolong her life, "You can't kill me because then you won't have the answers that you want."

"You don't know me," I retorted as I fired an arrow.

She caught it in mid-air just in front of her face.

I gasped with shock that quickly became confused annoyance.

Who is this woman?

Her eyes glinted as she retorted, "You don't know me either."

She jumped towards me and attacked me from every angle. I had to block every hit she made since I didn't want to come out injured like the last time I met her. Finally, I was able to grab her in a chokehold.

"Where is Cynthia Garcia? This is your last chance!" I shouted in her bulging eyes.

I asked once more, but she still did not relent.

Instead, she snatched a piece of glass from the floor and stabbed me right in the old shoulder wound.

I automatically let go and fell on my knees. The last thing I remember was her foot swiftly kicking me in the head.

I woke up back in my secret base. Emily had come to rescue me.

I shook my head in frustrated dismay, "I can't beat her. She knows more fight moves that I do."

"Don't beat yourself up too much. You are well-trained and you can beat her because you have a fire of goodness in you. We will find your Cynthia and my husband," Emily encouraged me.

"At least I got the tracking device on her shoe. I think I lost part of my brain for that, but it should yield some information," I shook my throbbing head back and forth and groaned as I struggled to get off the bed.

Emily and I returned to our surveillance of the city through our computer system.

It was easy to spot the Black Canary, but she only seemed to be completing mundane tasks.

Finally, on the fifth day, she went to an abandoned factory. Emily and I knew immediately that that was our chance. I quickly made my way to the factory and snuck inside.

I almost wept in happiness as I saw Cynthia sleeping in a cell. Yes, she was a prisoner, but she didn't look hurt. I could not take my eyes off her because I knew I was about to save her and we would be able to go home together.

I went to her cell to free her. I quietly woke Cynthia up. She looked so surprised but then teared up in happiness. It should have been the greatest shock in the world for her to see me alive after all these years. But in truth, it was like we had never been apart from each other. Our eyes were glistening with love for each other and I forgot that we were still in danger.

I was reminded of the danger by a blow to the back of my head. I was dizzy and confused, but I felt the dreaded Black Canary handcuff my hands, drag me somewhere, and chain me to a metal pipe in the ceiling.

When I regained my full consciousness, I realized that I was in a different room from Cynthia. The Black Canary came over to me and ripped my hood off my head.

But then, she did the unimaginable. She ripped off her hood.

It was the woman from the island.

So many questions darted in my mind.

How was she still alive?

How did she get off the island?

Why did she take Cynthia?

Why did she kill so many people?

I was so lost.

My mentor looked at me and said, "I know you have so many questions, but I need to stop you from what you're doing. I need to destroy this city because the people in this city sent me to the island. Nobody cares for me here. You need to say goodbye to everyone you love because you won't see them again. Roy, you have failed this city."

She left the room and I had a million more questions in my mind. But I quieted these thoughts and put all my energy into thinking about how to escape. I was even more invested in my crusade to truly fight violence and crime. I realized that she was a part of the problem, too.

I used the chains to pull myself up over the metal pipe and shimmied all the way down the pipe to where it was an open, exposed end. I slid my chained hands over the pipe and jumped down to freedom.

I immediately went to free Cynthia and took her to my home. My mom made a warm and safe bed for her and helped her shower and change into clean clothes. Cynthia was so exhausted and quickly fell asleep.

In my heart, I knew that the Black Canary planned to bomb the city in order to destroy the world that had caused her so much pain.

I returned to my secret base to reconnect with Emily because we had to save the city from the Black Canary's devious plans.

Emily searched the city and found the Black Canary depositing a bomb in a subway station. Emily immediately went to work hacking into the bomb's system and I ventured out into the city to capture this villain.

I knew she could kill me because I knew first hand of her skills.

I arrived at the subway station just as she was ascending the stairs. It was on!

We engaged in an epic battle of mentor and mentee where every move was taught and practiced, every move was thrown and blocked. We were exhausting each other, but neither of us would ever surrender.

The Black Canary grabbed her staff to hit me, but I blocked it with my bow. I fought back as she pulled out a dagger and stabbed my already injured shoulder. Nausea and black stars overwhelmed me as I fell to the floor.

"You can't beat me, Roy, because you don't know what you're fighting for. But I do!" she growled as she stepped on my shoulder to push the dagger in farther. I screamed in pain as she grabbed me in a chokehold. But the proximity gave me a chance to tear the dagger from my own shoulder and stab her in her neck with it. It was a mortal blow. I disentangled myself from her, but quickly my compassion for my mentor took me over.

I held her dying form and used my sleeve to wipe the blood from the corner of her mouth.

I looked deep into her eyes and said, "Thank you for teaching me what I'm fighting for and for helping me ensure that my father's death was not in vain."

Even though everything had become so complicated, my conscience was clear. I had done everything for her — I had given her food when she needed it on the island and I had killed every person on her list in the real world.

I had done some of the worst things imaginable, but it was over and the Canary was dead. The city of Los Angeles was safe.

I returned to life with my family and rekindled my relationship with Cynthia, whom I later married. Sometimes I watch her making supper and I feel this calm sense of normalcy and peace in my daily life. But then my ears catch something on the news and I know someone needs saving. That is when I don the Black Hood and venture out into the night into this twisted city that still needs saving. The Man in the Black Hood looks after this city and looks after the people he loves.

19

Los Angeles Civil War

By

Juan Rivera

On a sunny day on 108th and Compton, two Crips wearing blue, ironed shirts, baggy khaki pants, and blue shoes kept on the lookout for arrivals from the Bloods, Florence 13, or any other Compton or Watts gang.

With their eyes as red as a fat kid's fingers after he devoured hot Cheetos, they bantered about how to get the new black ops game that had just been released.

"Aye cuz, let's go jack someone for the new black ops," one suggested.

"Man, why you always gotta bring up jacking someone, Jason? We got enough dough to buy it ourselves," the other responded.

"Man, I told you not call me that, Josephina. My name is Little Killa," he said.

"Aight then, fool. Don't call me Josephina. My name is Joseph, aka Big Killa," Josephed retorted.

"Man shut up, cuz. Let's go buy it cuz. I'm bored," Little Killa said.

"Foshoo, let me just hit up the homeboy No Hesitation for a ride," Big Killa added.

Little did they know that this would spark a revolution.

***

Later that day, I forgot about the game and hit up my side chick. We chilled on the porch as we talked, smoked, and each drank four bottles of forties.

I woke up without my hoe and hungover the next day around noon. I rolled over and squinted my eyes to check my phone. Big Killa had texted me:

"Eye man, wya fool we finna be lit later man 50 grams of weed shoot thru at my party later."

I was surprised that he had invited me to go because I never really go to parties, only kickbacks. When I got to the party, I saw my hoe and I got mad because I didn't tell her to go to the party — someone else invited her. I got high and drunk so I forgot about her.

The next day, we were back on the porch chilling, smoking blunts, and drinking forties. It was a humid day and I suddenly remembered about the game.

"Ey cuhh, what happened to the game?" I asked.

"Lil K, what you mean 'what happen to the game,' cuz? You got busy with your hoe yesterday. You forgot. No Hesitation was here and you wasn't. So, we left to get the weed and the drinks for the party," he told me.

"Man, c'mon, cuz. Let's go get the game," I suggested.

"Ight, cuz. No Hesitation left his car yesterday cuz he was too drunk to drive," Big Killer told me.

"Foshoo, let's go," I said with excitement.

"Aight, we out," he said as we started for the car.

We went to go look for where No Hesitation had parked his badass muscle car. When we started the engine, it sounded like roaring thunder as we peeled out for the ten-minute drive to the game store.

"Aye man, this car is lit, cuz," Big Killa said.

"On crip, cuz. How he get this much money to buy this car?" I asked.

"Ion even know, cuz. Sh*t, he probably stole it."

"Ahh, who cares? Let's get back at my crib."

"Ight, Lil K. First, let's go get something to eat really quick."

"Foshoo, let's go buy some Panda Express, cuz. It's right around the corner."

After we ate the salty, oily, fantastic Panda Express, we went to my crib and played Black Ops Two. We demolished zombies and other online gamers who had dared to battle us.

When Big K left for his crib, I continued playing. In the online forum, this white kid kept talking sh*t. At first, I could not care less; but then he crossed the line.

"Aye, cuz, stop shanking, white boy," I typed.

"Hahaha, you're mad because you niggers don't know anything and you all keep talking smack on here but won't do nothing," he baited.

"On crip, cuz. If I say I'ma do something — best believe it finna happen, cuz."

"Hahaha, all you niggers are afraid of the cops. And, my dad is a cop."

"Yo dad ain't sh*t, cuz. You isn't finna do anything but run your mouth."

"Aye nigger, I bet if I knew where you lived I would go down there and kill your worthless self."

"You ain't gone do sh*t cuz. I live on 108th and Compton. My house is the blue one. Come do something, white boy."

I sat relaxed, but slightly vigilant.

The white boy didn't do anything, so I feel asleep.

The next day was a chill, sunny day. I smoked with my brother, Big K, and the homies. The day passed in a haze and I realized that it was ten at night and it had become foggy. My homeboys were outside smoking, and Big K was on the street popping fireworks.

SCREECHING car tires. GUN SHOTS!

A drive by — I ran to get my AK-47 and ran outside to see what had happened. As the drivers peeled away, I saw that my brother had been wounded.

"Who did this?" I heard my words fall into a sea of nothingness.

"Who did this!?" I shouted louder as I held my brother upright.

My words ricocheted off the walls of the neighboring apartment building like bullets.

"I never seen him before, cuz. He was a white boy driving a nice car," Big Killa said.

"Did he shoot my brother?" I asked.

"No, cuhh, he ran your brother over. That's when we shot and the white boy," one of the homies said.

I looked down at my brother. He was struggling to breath and white foamy liquid was coming out of his mouth. I held him upright so he could breathe better, but he only took a few more breaths and slumped lifelessly into my chest.

***

All the Los Angeles Crips were at my brother's funeral because we were well known in the gang. Even the leader came to pay his respects and to vent his anger. I knew who had killed my brother; but I didn't want to tell them because I wanted to go kill the son of a bitch with my own hands. My eyes narrowed in concentrated purposefulness as they lowered my brother's young body into the ground.

When I got home, I texted the white boy:

"Now you really f*cked up, cuz im coming for you, so be ready."

He messaged me back:

"What! I didn't do anything! I told my dad on your black ass and he said he was going to take care of it."

Of course that coward would try to deny this. I didn't believe him, so I started my hunt to find him. I asked the homeboys about what car they had seen that night. It was a white Benz. I asked my other homeboy to go into my ops game record and trace back to find out where the white boy lived.

"Aye, cuz, strap up. We finna go kill this white boy that killed my brother," I vowed.

"Let's go, cuz," Big Killa agreed. We went for the door.

We trolled the streets and kept our eyes open for the white Benz until we found the one — the front bumper was still dented from running down my brother. That arrogant ass was just driving around the car that had killed my brother!

We trailed him only to see him pull into the local liquor store where all the Feds buy liquor.

"Aye, cuz, he a cop. Let's head out before sh*t gets too heated," I said.

"Aight, Little K, sorry man," Big Killa said.

"What for, cuz? You ain't do nothing."

When we pulled onto my block, the whole area was filled with my homies who were bustling to tell me that someone was looking for me. I wiped the sweat off my brow — it was a humid, foggy night. I could sense an enemy was in our midst.

"Who here?" I asked suspiciously.

"He a crab, cuz. He said he wanted to talk to you about your brother," my homie relayed the message about the Blood gang member looking for me.

"Why didn't y'all just shoot his ass!?" I stammered.

"He ain't armed and he came alone. He said all he wanted to do was talk to you," the homie said.

The crowd of my homies parted and I walked closer to the Blood. I was infuriated as I saw him chilling and sitting at a table just having a drink.

I grabbed his shirt and pulled his face up to mine. I wanted to spit in his face and thrash him.

"Whoa, chill, cuz. We heard about your brother. I'm here to make a peace treaty between the Bloods and Crips in South Los Angeles," he said.

"Why you think we allies?" I fumed.

"Cuz, we all been suffering the police brutality against blacks and browns. We gotta join," he said.

I released his shirt and he calmly sat back in his seat. He raised the bottle of liquor and indicated that he wanted to share a drink with me.

I begrudgingly sat down and called for a glass, which my homie brought over to me. The Blood filled both our glasses and toasted as we both downed the shot.

We got down to talking business about the peace treaty and about how to deal with these corrupt cops. Around midnight, a car pulled up and the Blood got in and they drove away.

We all had a lot to think about.

***

After a few days passed, no one got into fights because of gang problems, except for all the Cholos. We kept meeting up to make a plan on how to stop the cops, then a bald Mexican with a long white t-shirt came up to us. His neck was tatted with *Florence*, his forehead with *F13*, and his knuckles with dates. He had *Rest in Peace* and various other designs tatted on his arms.

He put his right hand into his jacket packet and pulled out a Glock. We both thought we were going to die. He told us to go outside where we found a whole group of Bloods and Crips lying on the floor. They were being held at gunpoint and some were praying.

I turned to my friend and said, "Well, this is it, cuz. We finna die."

He laughed as he said, "And by a Mexican Blood, no less. I never thought of dying this way."

"Aye, vatos. Shut up and stop talking!" the Mexican Blood with the Glock warned.

We all waited in the afternoon sun until the Mexican did whatever he had planned. How were we going to argue with that firepower?

Finally, three low riders pulled up. Each one had a sticker for their territories of Florence, Watts, and Compton. When the drivers came out, all the Cholos aimed their weapons at the Bloods and

Crips. The Cholo that was guarding us told us to get up. We scrambled to our feet as I noticed that the men who had exited the car were approaching me.

Eight other men started to aim their guns at the Mexican Blood and myself. Things were getting tense. When the one with Florence came up to me, he pulled his shirt up and showed me a name tatted on his body. I read it but it did not ring a bell.

The guy eyed me up and asked, "Do you know who this is, homes?"

I thought it was someone we had killed, so I got scared.

I looked down at the ground and said, "No, cuz. I don't know who that is."

He replied with a steely tone, "It's my little brother's name, homes. The f*cking pigs shot him for no reason. He was just walking down the street and they pulled their guns on him. In a sec, he was gone. I heard what y'all was doing and we wanted to lend you a hand."

I was relieved and asked, "What's up with all the guns then, cuzz?"

"We wanted to show y'all what we can do to help if we all join together for once. I don't like these niggas from Compton and Watts, but we are willing to join together to end this discrimination from the feds," he added matter-of-factly.

"A'ight. Then can you tell these niggas to put the guns down?"

After this confrontation, the three Cholos helped Bryan, the Blood, and I come up with a plan to end the unfair treatment from the cops. At first, we thought of a peaceful protest. So, some Cholos, Bloods, and Crips went to the sheriff's department to do a protest march. When they got there, the sheriff and his deputies opened fire at them. They killed two Cholos, one Blood, and one Crip. They arrested other protestors and basically shut the whole thing that had intended to be peaceful with extreme violence.

In the news report, the sheriffs said that the protestors were posing a threat to the peaceful community. We all felt furious because our people had been unarmed and had only intended this to be a peaceful protest.

So, we took another course of action. Around 4 am the next morning, at least 250 gang bangers congregated on our block. When I got in my car, everyone else got in their cars and followed me. We got to the sheriff's department about a half hour later as dawn was breaking. Just Bryan, the three main Cholo leaders, and I got out of our cars and created a line. The others just waited in their cars.

After the bloodbath from the day before, the Feds were expecting us. So, they all rushed out and pointed their guns at us. But we did not flinch and we held our ground in a new form of a peaceful protest. The weather was hot and gloomy and every second was felt more and more like a Texas stand-off.

The sun beat down on our glistening faces until the sheriff finally broke the silence with a chuckle as he said, "We were expecting you. Now you are surrounded and you have lost, you niggers and immigrants."

I was not taking any of his racist flack and I responded, "Aye, cuz. Shut up with all this talking. You're all corrupt and we can't let you stay in power."

"Ohh, yeah, nigger. What you going to do about it?" was his intellectual reply.

I was more than ready for him and replied, "Well, you may have a small army, but I have a military."

After I said that, all the throngs of the Cholos and gangbangers got out of their cars and made a formation behind the five of us. The cop was sweating with fear and he started shaking. He then gave the order to the other officers to aim their guns at us.

As soon as the cops aimed their guns at us, all the Cholos and gangbangers pulled out their weapons, which ranged from pistols to rocket launchers. The tension could have been cut with a knife as everything boiled over into palpable tension.

One of the young rookie cops got too scared and shot at the Florence gang leader who was there to get revenge for his brother's murder.

"You shot my brother!" the wounded Florence leader shouted with anger as he recognized the cop who had murdered his brother. With that, it was open season and everybody behind me opened fire. Bullets raged with anger and pulverized the cops.

After all the years of abuse we had suffered, none of us felt the need to show mercy. When all the officers outside the police station were dead or on the ground, the gangbangers strode across the blood splattered concrete and ascended the station stairs.

Like animals in a jungle, the cops had organized their station so they would have the higher ground to stop any attackers and to attack themselves.

There were about ten sheriffs left in the department. We easily overwhelmed them and killed them all. They looked like slaughtered animals when we were done.

We all checked the whole station looking for any more cops. Suddenly, I found the cop who had started the whole gun battle outside, sniveling under a large desk. He had somehow managed to sneak back into the station to hide and wait out the fight.

I grabbed him by the scruff of his neck and dragged him out for everyone to see.

The Florence gang leader said, "Let this pig go. Let him snitch on us. We need to get reputation that we aren't playing around anymore."

I thought it was a dumb idea so I pulled out a Glock 9 and pointed it at his head.

"We went through all of this to specifically kill this guy. And, you finna let him go?" I stammered in annoyance.

The Cholo said, "Yeah, homes. We need to strike fear in the government's heart."

As I thought about it, I decided that it might be smart. But I was about to find out just what a bad idea it was for our whole community.

About three weeks after the siege on the sheriff station, we saw on the news that the government had learned of our identities and our involvement in the massacre. At first, they said that they were going to move in troops to stop the madness that was going on around the hood.

When they showed up, we had the entire city of South Los Angeles — from the highest criminals to the homeless people from the streets — on our side. The protest was epic.

The cops started arresting the innocent marchers and shooting tear gas into the crowds. Little kids were crying and screaming as people started running for safety.

Brian surveyed the chaos and said to me, "Aye, cuz. Let's tell everyone to bounce before it gets worse."

"Foreall, vato. We have to come up with something to make them stop harassing and killing us," I added.

The next morning was gloomy and foggy and the grass was sprinkled with raindrops. Bryan, the three Cholos, and I had spent the whole night coming up with a plan to prevent anyone else from getting hurt. When we had devised a plan, we called in the cavalry.

I stood in front of the whole crowd of people who were unified for peace and said, "I'm going to turn myself in to the cops."

Everyone gasped and a murmur of disagreement rose from the crowd.

"Aye, homes. This wasn't part of the plan," one of the Cholos said in disbelief.

"On me, Blood. Why you finna turn yourself in?" another one asked.

"It's the only way that they'll stop bothering everyone. I'll take the blame for the entire sheriff's shooting," I said with humility.

They all disagreed with me, but I held firm to my decision.

The next morning I went to the police station and turned myself in. A little group of Cholos and gangbangers wanted to break me out of the cop car that was transporting me to another station. They shot the driver and they took me out.

"Run! Leave!" I shouted to them. "I want to do this — it's the only way we can finally have peace in this damned city!"

The next day, I was in court and found the entire place was filled with Cholos and gangsters.

"Yes, your honor. I am responsible for the shootings at the sheriff's office and for organizing the large protest," I quietly said to the judge.

I took the blame for everything, but the case stretched out longer than anyone expected.

The judge asked me, "Why did you do it?"

Everyone knew me as a hard core gangbanger who did not care about how anyone else felt. I was known for having a heart filled with ice, but this time I could not hold in the pain of all the losses we had suffered.

Tears streamed down my cheeks as I answered the judge. I found myself crying for the lost lives and for all the people who had suffered police discrimination. I cried for all the senseless deaths of my black and brown brothers, especially for the death of my brother Big K.

I entreated the judge and said, "We're all tired of being treated like animals. We're people who have rights and feelings. My brother got ran over by a Fed for no reason. He was standing outside when this nigga decided to run him over."

After I finished telling my story, the judge decided to take my statements all the way to the President of the United States because we were not the only community facing discrimination from the Feds — it was all over Los Angeles, and all over America.

President Obama did indeed take notice of what had happened in my neighborhood. He revamped the police departments by retraining the cops and instituting stricter regulations for police brutality. I was sentenced to four years in jail, but he reduced my sentence to only one year.

When I was released from jail, everyone in L.A. knew my name. And, when I returned to my hood, I found several news channels all clamoring to interview me. I could tell that some of the journalists were just flattering me to get the story they needed. And, others just tried to get up in my face and get me to react and cause a scene. But I was a man of peace and a man at peace. So none of these people could ruffle my feathers.

I do remember one guy who asked me, "What kind of nigger would go to a sheriff's department and shoot everyone there for another nigger?"

I chuckled at his rude question and responded with the wisdom that this whole experience had endowed me with, "The one that got recognized by the president."

There were not anymore problems in the hood. All of the Bloods, Crips, Cholos, and other gangs helped each other and there were no more conflicts between the blacks and browns. The L.A. crime rate dropped by 95%.

One sunny day, I was chilling on my porch while drinking an Arizona Ice Tea and eating a burger. I heard a whirling sound from the sky and looked up to see the leaves and branches of the shady tree above me swirling around in the powerful winds.

Suddenly, I saw four military helicopters fly directly over my house.

My heart jumped into my throat as I thought that I might be being arrested again and taken back to jail. Sure enough, the helicopter hovered in the air in a circle around my house.

Then, more noise filled the air as the ground began to shake. I put down my tea and half-eaten burger as I saw about half of the L.A. police department, two tanks, two military trucks, a long black limousine, two more tanks, two military trucks, and (what looked like) the rest of L.A. police department. The convoy rolled passed me as I stood in wonder. Finally, they stopped as the black limousine came to my house's walkway.

When the car stopped, twenty-five agents swiftly exited their cars and stood at attention in different strategic positions. I wiped any ketchup off my mouth with a napkin. Yeah, something big was going on.

A security agent opened the limo door and President Barack Obama cheerfully came out of the car.

I was shocked, to say the least, to see the President in the hood.

"Are you…" his voice cracked like if he was trying to remember something. "Uhhh, are you the person they call Lil K?" he asked me.

I responded with fear in my voice, "Yes, sir. My name is actually Jason. I don't use that old name anymore."

"Probably a good idea," he said with a smile as he shook my hand. "Michelle and I have been very impressed with what you did here. You made everyone's lives safer and better," he said as he handed me an envelope that said United Airlines on it.

I just looked down with embarrassment. I had never set out to do these things, but I was happy that I had made my brother's death lead to protecting other people's brothers and sisters. President Obama invited me to an all-expense-paid trip to the White House where he presented me with the Presidential Medal of Freedom.

From then on, I continued to dedicate my life to preventing violence in my neighborhood, my state, my country, and my world.

20

A Boy Achieving His Goals

By

Thomas Arreaga

Chapter 1

Tony strained his neck peering out the foggy bus windows looking for his stop. An annoying stranger was holding onto the overhead railing between the exit doors blocking Tony's view.

"Excuse me, can you move over because I can't see where I'm getting off at," Tony said to the stranger.

"Sorry, I didn't see there," said the stranger as he moved out of the way.

With the clear view, Tony saw what he thought he should be seeing — his stop was next. He jumped off the bus with relief that he had not missed his stop and promptly pulled out his phone to check his messages. His girlfriend had texted him to ask where he was at.

He quickly texted her that he had just arrived and was on his way to class.

As Tony entered the school, he rushed past the boards where his name was listed in the straight A, honor roll groups for every semester. He wiped the sweat off his brow not just because he was hurrying but because he was getting more nervous about the test for his university scholarship applications that he was about to take.

He went to the bathroom and splashed some water on his face and stared at himself in the mirror.

You can do this.

With his confidence renewed, he boldly walked into his homeroom and said, "Ms. Lopez, I'm ready to take the test."

She gave him and the other students their exams and the whole process started as the students hunched their backs over their desks in concentration.

Tony immersed himself in the test and flew through each question and answer.

"Time's up!" Ms. Lopez announced to the class of students.

Some groaned in disappointment, but Tony knew he had to hurry and get over to his guidance counselor.

He thanked Ms. Lopez, who smiled happily at him as she took his exam and put it on the stack with the other hopeful students.

At the guidance office, Tony looked through the glass to see Ms. Mata working on her computer. He knocked on the glass and she waived him in.

"How was your test?" she asked.

"It was good. You know you always wish you had more time," Tony answered. "I'm just here to double check that I have all the credits I need to graduate and to fulfill the scholarship requirements."

Ms. Mata typed in Tony's first and last name and pulled up his academic file. As she ran her fingertip up and down the Excel file with four years' worth of grades and teacher comments, Tony felt his breathing get faster.

What if there is something missing? What if? What if…

"Tony, everything looks good. As far as I can see, you're right on track," Ms. Mata said with a satisfied look on her face.

"Perfect," Tony said with a sigh of relief as he grabbed his bag to go. "Thank you for always looking out for me," he added as he left.

Tony walked down the halls as his mind retraced so many milestones that he had crossed to get to this level of completing his high school studies.

Tony pushed open the school doors to the grassy outdoor area where the students liked to relax and eat lunch. He spied his girlfriend Rosa sitting under their favorite tree. He waived to her and he made his way through the pockets of picnicking students. Tony thought Rosa looked beautiful with her long, dark brown hair fluttering in the breeze.

"How was your test?" Rosa asked as she pecked Tony on the check.

"Good, the time flew by!" he said as he situated himself on the grass and pulled out a squished peanut butter and jelly sandwich from his backpack.

"Babe, what college are you thinking about going to?" Rosa asked, as she bit into a dark red apple.

"You know I want to know where you're going so we can go to the same school. We can decide once we know which schools have accepted both of us," he said with a smile and stole another kiss from her.

In his heart, Tony hoped that the schools with strong soccer teams accepted both of them. Tony was a tall guy, so everyone always encouraged him to play basketball; but he knew his true passion was soccer. He wanted to become a top player on an international team.

One of the things he loved most about Rosa was that she supported him in his dreams.

Tony and Rosa finished their lunches and both went their separate ways to attend their afternoon classes. After school, Tony played soccer with the guys and then practiced kicking goals on his own. He loved the solitude of kicking goal after goal. He could hear the whisper of the ball passing just centimeters below the top of the goal post as the imaginary goalkeeper dove in vain to catch the ball. The crowd always roared.

Tony did not get home until around 8 pm that night and his parents angrily accosted him at the door.

"Where were you? Why didn't you call? You're so irresponsible. We just can't take this anymore!" his parents went on and on.

Tony did an about face and went back to his car. In the driver's seat, he texted Rosa and he could not help the tears from falling. He knew his parents were on the verge of kicking him out of the house.

Thoughts about finding somewhere to live where no one knew him or could bother him played on a loop in his mind.

Rosa called him and asked, "Where you at, babe?"

"I'm just riding around to go get food. My parents are hassling me about the same old problems," he answered as he tried to hide his weeping voice.

"Come and pick me up," Rosa said. "I'll stay with you until you find a safe place to stay."

Tony ditched his plans to buy food and went to get Rosa, who was waiting by the curb when he pulled up to her house. She was his rock.

Tony and Rosa went to a fancy restaurant where they could sneak food from the back of the house because Tony's friend worked there.

They sat on the steps at the back entrance of the restaurant eating the forgotten doggie bag from clients who had not finished half their steak or pasta primavera.

"Don't worry, sweetheart," Rosa said as she leaned her head on Tony's shoulder. "You can stay at my house," she added.

"Where's he going to stay?" half-shouted Rosa's mom.

"He can stay in one of my brother's beds," Rosa said as she pulled a fresh blanket down from the closet.

As Tony went to sleep for the first time in a house filled with love, he meditated on the big soccer game that was tomorrow morning.

Chapter 2

Tony slept better than he expected and he woke up bright and early for the match against Lancaster.

He went to Rosa's room and knocked on the door.

"Rosa?" he said with urgency as he looked down at his watch.

"Yes?" she answered.

"Are you coming to the game?"

"Of course. I'll be ready. I'll meet you in the kitchen. My mom's making breakfast for us and then she'll drive us. Did you check the weather?"

"Sounds good. Let me look out the window," Tony said as he pulled back the curtains.

"Oh, no. It's snowing," he said with worry to Rosa.

Rosa came out of her bedroom. She had half her pajamas on and half her day clothes. She too looked out the window and grimaced.

"Let's leave now," Rosa said with determination.

Rosa's mom drove through the snow, which was light for places where the people are used to the snow. But in Los Angeles people freak out over the little bits of rain or snow.

The traffic was terrible. Tony struggled to dress in the back of the car and they all dropped more of their Egg McMuffins than they ate on the drive.

At the Lancaster field, it was just as Tony has expected. Tony's club managers had brought scouts to watch them play as an informal tryout for the pros. Tony knew that this was his big chance to get out of this horrible life of financial stress.

Tony tried to avoid staring at the scouts as he fell into formation with his teammates to do some warm-up exercises. The other team was doing the same and Tony began scanning them to gauge their overall strength and their sense of teamwork.

But as he scanned the scouts, opposition, and the growing crowd, he noticed his dad in the bleachers.

What was he doing there? He's probably bragging to his friends about me. Yeah, you jerk. You brag about me to your friends, but you treat me like dirt at home. Why don't you tell your friends about

where I stayed last night, huh?

Tony used this fire of anger to kick the ball harder and faster than he ever had. He could feel the energy of the crowd spurring him on. He sensed the scouts watching his every move and making notes in their books. Finally, at halftime, one of the scouts went to the coach and clearly initiated a conversation about Tony as they kept glancing over at him. Eventually, the coach called Tony over.

"Son, this is Coach Jonas from Barcelona. He'd like to talk with you about your future plans," Tony's coach explained.

Tony tried to maintain a respectful tone but hid his sheer joy. This was one of the best teams in the world.

The coach looked at Tony and explained, "You can take five members of your family or friends to help support you. Think it over for the rest of the game. The coaches will make their offers at the game end."

Tony ran back to the field. He tried to block all of that information out of his mind, as he played even better than before.

Of course, Tony's team won and all the team players who were interested in contracts lined up to be picked by different scouts. The first scout picked TJ, a slow kid who was a midfielder. The French scout picked a strong defender to join PSG. Of course, the European scout confirmed that he wanted Tony and handed him a package with all the departure information.

Tony's hands were shaking with excitement, but his thoughts quickly turned to making sure that Rosa could also fulfill her dream of visiting the beautiful city of Barcelona and of seeing her favorite team Barca play.

Chapter 3

"You know I want to go," Rosa said sadly. "But it's too much money. I have to stay here to work and help my family."

"Babe, the team will pay for everything. Come with me and I'll be able to set us up for life. You know I want to take care of you," Tony encouraged her.

Rosa seemed to be mulling it over, so Tony turned his attention to his friends Bell, Isaac, and David to let them know that they all were being offered the opportunity of a lifetime.

The days flew by and it was time for Tony and his entourage to leave for the airport. They boarded the airport shuttle and Tony looked at Rosa and all his friends with love. He had known that all those hours of hard practice were going to pay off. And here was the payday.

At the airport, Tony and his friends sat to eat before the flight. Suddenly, Tony felt his phone in his pocket vibrate. He pulled out the phone to check the number and found that it was from an unlisted number. Tony worried that it was someone from the team and that he should take the call.

He dialed the number back and who should be on the other end but his mom. She was sobbing that she did not want him to leave for a faraway place. Tony's blood pressure jumped through the roof. Deep in his heart, Tony felt that she only wanted access to his future earnings from football. They had had years to show him kindness and love and this was not going to cut it.

But if Tony thought he was mad, he had no idea how mad Rosa was going to be. She snatched the phone from Tony's hand and put the receiver up to her mouth.

"Don't call him again," Rosa said emphatically and hung up the phone.

Rosa immediately called her own mother who jumped on the phone and talked to Tony in order to call him down. No one wanted Tony to be lost in emotions as he set out on this new adventure in his life.

Chapter 4

Tony and his friends enjoyed the plane ride and made themselves cozy in their adjoined seats. When Rosa fell asleep, Tony motioned to Isaac, Bell, and David to meet him at the back of the plane.

They all quietly made their way to the open space near the emergency exit door. Tony unburdened himself about the stress of his family life.

"It's okay, buddy. You know we are all going to be here when you need help," Bell immediately answered, as Isaac and David nodded in agreement.

Tony smiled, not just on his face, but in his heart because of these kind words from his true friends.

Tony went back to his seat and sat down next to the slumbering Rosa. He thought about when they had first started dating and he went to meet Rosa's mom. He did not know how to act in the house filled with Rosa's brothers playing tag and all the loving chaos of a happy family. Rosa's mother had obviously sensed Tony's discomfort and asked him to go with Rosa to the store to get some watermelon.

Of course they went and when they brought it back, the dining room table was set with enchiladas and salad. They all ate like a family and Tony helped Rosa do the dishes. He knew he should be doing all these things, but he really felt like doing them and he hoped it showed.

Later that night, Rosa, her brothers, and her father all settled in to watch Barca play and Rosa's mom had called him to kitchen.

"Tony, can you help me serve the watermelon?" she asked.

"Of course," he said as he

Tony told Rosa's mom all the love he had for her daughter and that he had never known a girl who liked soccer.

That day they landed at the Barcelona airport to meet the scouter at his home. Tony, Rosa, and Rosa's mom were happy to be in Barcelona because it was their first time there. The scouter's house was magnificent and had a swimming pool, pool table, plasma TV, video game library — it had everything that Tony dreamed of having. Tony's friends were surprised because Tony had achieved his dream. Rosa was happy for Tony for making it this far in his aspiration to be a professional soccer player and that they could be together.

Rosa ran up to Tony and hugged him, and then she started to kiss him and kept saying that she loved him. She was crying with emotion because she had believed in Tony the whole time. Tony wiped the tears off of Rosa's face with the sleeve of his sweater and kissed her.

"Tony!" his friends yelled from the second floor.

"I'm coming," Tony said in tense voice because he wanted to be with Rosa.

Rosa told Tony, "I'll go with you to see the rooms."

They all explored the scouter's amazing house and started to play the various video games on the PlayStation 4, PlayStation 3, Xbox 1, Xbox 360, and the old systems, too.

Chapter 5

Saturday morning was Tony's first game with the Barcelona team when they planned to test his skills.

He felt truly challenged and truly alive because he had only played average players before, but now he was in a top, international team. He gave it all he had the whole game because he wanted to impress his coach and the whole crowd. When he scored a goal, Rosa and her mom cheered for him from the VIP area where they had their choice of delicious snacks.

"Barca, Barca, Barca!" all the fans cheered because it was a championship match and Barcelona was in first place. Tony stole the ball from an opponent only to be fouled by a cheeky player who hit Tony in the back. Rosa gasped when she saw the hard hit that Tony suffered. The referee had called a free kick so Tony had another chance to impress his coaches and show his love for Rosa, whom he imagined was the winner of each of his goals.

Tony calmed down for his shot and looked for an angle to score for the last minute goal. The referee blew the whistle for the kick, so Tony kicked the ball to the top corner goal post where the keeper couldn't reach it. But it hit the pole and fans groaned because they thought he had lost the chance to score. However, everyone shouted in excitement when the ball bounced across the goal into the net. It was an amazing goal and the whole crowd for Barcelona went wild.

"GGGOOOAAALLL," the announcers shouted over the din.

"Tony, Tony, Tony!" all the fans shouted in exuberant excitement. Rosa left the VIP box and went down to go congratulate Tony on the goal that he had scored for her. But people crowded around Tony, who could see Rosa reaching for him beyond the crowd. He felt a deep desire to find a perfect gift for her to show his appreciation for all the support she had given him in the past months.

Finally, the crowd around Tony dispersed and Rosa rushed in to hug Tony and to congratulate him for the goal. But as Rosa held him, Tony began to have chills and he began to feel a strange sense of anxiety and dread. He started breathing deeply and then hyperventilating. His head was throbbing and his body hurt all over. His mind was racing a million miles an hour as he looked into Rosa's worried eyes.

"I don't think I can play soccer anymore," Tony said to the complete shock of everyone around him.

Chapter 6

Rosa held Tony's hand as he cried in frustration because he wanted to return to playing soccer and continue on his journey to being a pro-athlete.

"I don't want to finish like this," he sobbed in anger.

"Tony, it's not over. You've made me so happy. I felt your love every time you scored a goal for me," she said in a tone tinged with concern and sadness.

Tony rested his head back on the sofa and knew what he needed to do. He needed to face these medical issues.

"Rosa, will you take me to the hospital?" he asked.

"Of course, my love. Let me call for an appointment," she said with relief.

"No, just take me now. I feel so much pain and my head hurts," Tony said.

He just could not maintain the façade of strength any more. But he knew he could count on Rosa to help him and to stay by his side.

Rosa took Tony to the ER and filled out the paperwork to have him checked over.

They held hands as they waited in the ER with people holding bloody bandages on various body parts. Tony had no cuts on his body, but he could feel himself weakening even as he sat there.

"Tony," a nurse with a clipboard called out.

Tony immediately tried to stand but fell back into the seat.

"What's wrong?" Rosa asked with worry as she took him by his upper arm and tried to help Tony stand.

Tony slumped down in the seat with resignation and said," I don't think I can walk."

"What are you talking about? You just walked in here," Rosa said with confusion.

"All of my energy is gone. I just can't walk," Tony said in a listless voice.

The nurse silently listened to the whole conversation and went to fetch a wheelchair. She and Rosa helped the enervated Tony to settle into the seat. He held his head in his hand and covered his eyes as the nurse rolled him through the hospital doors to an examination room.

Tony became depressed as the doctors performed a battery of tests on his weakened body. An MRI revealed that he had suffered a brain injury as well as several other injuries. He was paralyzed from the waist down and became less independent with every passing day.

"When did you have a brain injury?" Rosa asked with mounting confusion.

"When I was little," Tony quietly answered without offering any details.

Tony became lost in nightmares about the past. Rosa sat vigil while he tossed and turned on his bed as the smell of cold sweat permeated the room. He would just mutter for hours and Rosa became increasingly worried.

"Please, please, my love," said Rosa. "Please be strong for our future, for our future children."

Tony spent the days sitting in his wheelchair and looking out the window. He barely tried to get stronger when doing his physical therapy exercises. He lost his will to fight.

At the hospital, the doctor asked Rosa and Tony's friends what had happened to Tony.

"He played yesterday for the Barcelona game; however, he hit the ball with his head a lot of times," Rosa answered.

The doctor told them that Tony had a traumatic head injury that had made his mind lost in the past — a past that seemed filled with trauma. Rosa could not believe that a human mind could have that type of reaction in the brain.

Rosa asked the doctor, "What can I do to make him confident again?"

"Well, you can do what you're already doing — just be there for him," the doctor said in a voice that was assuring and optimistic.

Tony was discharged from the hospital and Rosa was waiting for him with his friends. Rosa had tried to bolster Tony's confidence to help him play soccer again. Rosa's mom even tried to help out by talking to him about how he had already achieved his dream and now he just had to live it. This was going to support his and Rosa's life and allow them to provide everything for their future children.

Slowly but surely, all these kind words of love and encouragement eased Tony's pain and his confidence grew day by day. Rosa took Tony to the gym where it had all started for him and she acted as his coach and his confidante. Rosa's own confidence built during this time as she grew from a teenager into a young woman, who could become a strong wife and mother. Tony's return to the Barca playing field was hailed as a triumph as he scored a goal. He was now a man who could grasp his dream with two hands and become a strong husband and father.

21

THE LAND UNKNOWN

By

Rruamdy Cruzuee

Chapter 1

It was the hottest and, luckily, the last day of summer. School, which annoyed my brother Kai but enthralled my brother Lee and me, was about to start the next day. Kai was crestfallen that his reprieve from academia was over, but I was excited that my last days of boring summer vacation were coming to a close.

I wandered into the house to find my mother making my favorite food, tortas cubanas. The mixture of spicy chorizo and other meats, an array of vegetables, and Chihuahua cheese made my mouth water and my taste buds explode.

I lay on my bed for just a few minutes while I waited for the tortas cubanas.

Suddenly, Lee was shaking me awake.

"Hey, it's time to get up for school," he said.

What? I was shocked on two levels — first; I slept through my favorite meal? Second, I was now a sophomore?

As my brothers and I made our way to school, I became acutely aware at our difference in height. I had sprung up like a skyscraper while they had remained like ants.

On the walk, Lee and I teased each other and play-pushed each other back and forth. But Kai lagged behind, lost in his own grumpy thoughts. I thought to myself how this was a physical metaphor of how Lee and I were in contrast to the Black Sheep Kai.

As I thought about how I had grown over the summer, I wondered about how different my friends would look after the summer. At the school entryway, Kai silently turned to go to his own homeroom.

"Xolten! Lee! There you guys are," I heard this shrimpy voice call to me above the noisy crowd.

I had to blink because at first I did not recognize my friend Acery. I had to laugh because this feisty chick looked even shorter than before, as Lee and I towered over her.

"Guys! Come on! The others are…" she tried to say before Lee and I cut her off.

"Where?" we asked simultaneously?

I couldn't wait to see the others and nearly hopped out of my own body from excitement. I could tell Lee felt my excitement. Finally, I went with Acery to meet the others. I nearly cried tears of happiness when I saw Sergio, Barry, and Citlalie.

I had not seen them since the start of summer and they had all changed so much. Sergio had gotten tall and buff. I was six feet, but I think he was now a few inches taller than I was. Barry also looked buff, but he looked lankier than strong. Citlalie had changed the most. She looked really emo with her tall, wispy form and her long hair.

I did not know what to say. I wanted to say many things, but no words came out of my mouth. I finally just grabbed them all and gave them a huge, long hug. After we had all caught up, we headed to our first class, which was chemistry.

I have loved science since I was a child and I always wished that I could invent something to change the world. But I had never had the chance to do something really amazing. We all settled into seats at the back of the class.

"Good morning class," a tall, strange man with a very deep voice uttered. "My name is Mr. Grim. I'll be your chemistry teacher for the rest of the year."

The teacher, who somehow exuded a sense of innocence, started a slide show about the class rules. The rest of the classes and the day went by like nothing. It was as if the feeling of freedom and excitement of summer vacation simply continued within our school world — I loved learning and immensely enjoyed my days.

We had general assignments and tests until one day something extraordinary happened. In History class, this guy and girl talked about how their company was looking for new scientific minds.

"We're holding a contest to find revolutionary inventions that will be judged five months from now. The winner receives a check for $300,000," the young man explained with gusto.

I could tell that everyone's minds were reeling just thinking about the money, but my mind reeled thinking about the possibility of inventing something that could change the course of human existence.

I, loving science, instantly came up with an idea for a machine that would shrink trash to a size smaller than that of atoms. I wanted to get my brother's friends in on the idea. So, at lunch, I immediately told them my idea and they all said they were on board, except Acery.

"Your idea is crap and you'll never win," she said with a gloomy anger.

Even though Acery was a good friend, she was always a stick in the mud. So, I just ignored her and turned back to explaining my idea to the others. After everybody else seemed enthusiastic about the idea, I turned my attention back to Acery. She could tell there was a fever of excitement and she relented.

"All right, I'll help you build your stupid machine," she said.

If that was the best Acery could do, I would accept it.

Later, I delegated different roles in invention building process to each person based on his or her skills. Sergio would get the parts; Lee would draw the machine; Citlalie would help me check out the calculations and decide what would go where; and Barry and Acery would make sure nothing went wrong with the overall process. I was ecstatic at the progress we had made in just a day. I had almost everything I needed to give life to my idea. My mind continued to race through thoughts of all the things I would need and each step of the plan.

At school the next day, I asked my crew if they knew of a large enough free space for us to work in to build the machine. Even though we would be creating a machine that would make things smaller, the physical machine would be quite large. Everyone was at a loss and a pall of disappointment descended on the group.

As we dispersed to attend classes, I walked the hallways with Acery who suddenly told me about this old warehouse near the school. I wondered why she did not tell me when the others were there. I pondered the question, but not for too long because I was thrilled that we had a construction site.

As soon as school let out, I ran to Acery's last class of the day so she could lead me to the warehouse.

"I'm not sure about this idea," she said to me. "I don't think you'll like the warehouse."

I was shocked and tried not to get annoyed at Acery's stalling tactic. Why was she saying this after she was the one who brought up the warehouse in the first place?

"Please, Acery. Just show me the place. This is my dream and my opportunity to do something helpful for people," I pleaded.

"All right, I'll show you tomorrow morning before school," she agreed.

She was always a puzzle, so I did not worry too much more about it. I was just excited that she had agreed to help out in this way.

In the pre-dawn hours, I left my house to meet up with Acery who met me in front of the school. We walked under the cover of darkness with our way lit by the glittering stars overhead.

"So, why did you run off so fast yesterday," I asked inquisitively.

"No reason," she replied in a low voice.

"Really, you sure?"

"Yes! Can we just walk over to the warehouse?"

"Okay, okay."

We continued to walk in the darkness without saying a single word to each other.

Once we arrived at the warehouse, it was nearly dawn. I hated to upset her, but this whole situation was too weird.

"Why are we coming to the warehouse so early without the others?" I gently asked.

"Sh, okay," she replied angrily. "Jeez, Xolten. I wanted you to see it before the others did. God, you're just so... I don't know, so...Just, shut up. Okay?" she said as if wanted to smack me up side my head.

Acery opened the back door of the warehouse, and we went inside where a cold, ominous vibe took over. It was like being in a dark cave. I could not see two steps in front of me until Acery turned on the lights. The warehouse lit up with life.

Out of the corner of my eye, I noticed a pile of clothes and what look like bed sheets. But before I could check it out, Acery yanked me away and showed me the rest of the warehouse. She showed me a great area to build our invention.

I was at a loss for words because the warehouse was so perfect for what we needed. I texted the others about it and I hugged Acery. As we hugged, I heard her utter some words that I could not distinguish. As we looked out the window, we saw that dawn was breaking.

We ran to school and our hearts were pounding by the time we got there. As we took a second to catch our breath, I noticed some of the others from our crew were arriving. I told them more about the warehouse and they all were excited to check it out. School passed in a second because my mind was filled with thoughts about how to create the invention and the wonderful impact it could have on the world.

Once school let out, I told the others where the warehouse was and we met up there. Everyone had all their parts ready. Lee had the drawing while and Barry and Acery had checked the calculations. Citlalie and I were still preparing our things that would be needed later. That day we put a lot of things together and made real progress. We had months to build our invention, but we were so motivated that we were well ahead of schedule.

As we all headed home for the night, I noticed Acery didn't leave the warehouse. It was the weekend and I worried about why it looked like she was sleeping in that cold place. I did not sleep well that Friday night as I tossed and turned, worrying about her.

But I still got up bright and early on Saturday to meet everyone at the warehouse to continue our plan. We joined pieces of metal and created a computer program to operate our machine. I felt so fortunate to have brilliant, dedicated friends.

We all joined together for the moment of putting in the last of the metal sheets to complete the project. I didn't know what to say, so I didn't say anything. I happily put the last piece in place and began the test on the first prototype. I flipped the switch to turn it on and I was overwhelmed with happiness.

Suddenly, the machine started to go haywire. The lights flashed red, white, blue, and purple as the laser on top started shooting everywhere. The laser, which was designed to shrink things, started shrinking everything it was striking. It was terrifying and we all ran for cover.

A loud BOOM shook the ground and my vision blurred. I could not hear anything nor could I see my friends clearly. I felt like some powerful force was sucking me as well as my friends into a vortex. As I got sucked in, I felt like dying. My thoughts raced as I lamented that my miniaturization machine had failed and I had hurt or even killed my friends. I was lost in thoughts of anger and frustration until I was jarred from these murky thoughts with a heavy thud of my body hitting solid ground.

Chapter 2: Me and My Idea

I awoke hoping it had all been a dream, but I was wrong. It was all too real. I staggered to my feet as a sharp pain flared from my hip that felt fractured. As I stood up, I saw no sign of my friends or my brother — I only saw mountains, trees, and a thick brush.

I couldn't wrap my head around what had happened.

Was this Earth? Was I dead?

I didn't have time to think about all these issues because I needed to find out if my friends were in the strange world as well. Luckily, I would not have to wait long.

"Anyone out there? Guys?" the voice cried out.

"Here!" I replied unsure if it was anyone I knew.

Suddenly, the short and shrimpy figure of Acery appeared.

She looked awful and must have suffered terribly during the vortex shift.

She approached me with a sigh of relief, "Xolten, I'm glad it's you. Are you okay?"

"Yeah, I'm fine. I'm just a bit bruised."

"Where are the others?"

"I don't know. But we'll find them. If you're here, then they must be here, too."

"But where is here?"

"I'm not sure. But I'm sure, we're on Earth."

"Really? Then, why is there a green cloud in the sky and two suns that glow blue? Xolten, I'm scared and I don't know if we'll ever see the others again."

"Hey, Acery, calm down. Don't cry. Everything will be okay and we'll find the others."

As we comforted each other, we heard the unmistakable voices of Sergio, Lee, Citlalie, and Barry. They were all trying to find us and trying to find out where we were.

Acery could not hold her excitement and zoomed over to them. She hugged them until they went limp. But after our initial excitement, the gravity of our situation returned.

"Xolten what's our next move?" Lee asked.

The others stared at me.

I did not know what to do so I tried to be honest and said, "Guys, I'm not sure. I don't know."

"What? But we thought you would know!" they all replied.

I was disappointed in myself because they had all trusted me.

Thud, thud — a great sound and vibrations interrupted our discussion.

"Guys what's happening?" I asked as we all looked around.

"I don't know," said Sergio.

"Oh, god," Barry said in a frightened tone.

"Are we gonna die?" Acery asked.

"Dear God," Lee exclaimed.

"Oh, my god!" Citlalie screamed.

Suddenly, a huge bear-like creature with horns burst out of the bushes.

ROAR!

"F*ck! Guys, run!" I screamed at my friends who were already running.

We all ran in the same direction since we did not want to get separated again. My hip on fire, but I ran through the pain until I tripped and fell on my face. Lee and everyone quickly turned back to help me — everyone except Barry.

"Barry!" I cried after him, but he was long gone.

My friends picked me up as the bear closed in. My heart was pounding in my chest and I felt like fainting. My legs were turning to Jell-O as the bear attacked me and tore at my side. I howled in pain as the predator ripped open my side like my body was an envelope.

Lee, Sergio, and Acery tried to fight it, but it just tossed them like paper dolls. We thought we had truly met our fate until something even stranger happened. An unfamiliar creature came out of nowhere and blasted the bear animal with some sort of orb. The bear creature dropped me and ran off as the stranger bombarded it with orbs. I fell into Citlali's arms as my life continued flash before my eyes.

"Thank you so much. You saved my life. What is your name?" I said to the helpful creature.

"There is no need, earthling. I saw you were in trouble and came to help. My name is xoxo bo, but in your language my name is pronounced as Quickster," he replied.

The others stepped closer to take a closer look at Quickster. Just moments before, everything had seemed so grim. I was about to be mauled to death and Barry, the coward, had abandoned me.

"Earthlings, would you like me to help you find your friend?" I heard Quickster ask.

"No!" I screamed. "I hope Barry rots in hell after he left me to die!"

"I do not understand what this 'coward' word means," Quickster said.

I was beyond frustrated and just had to walk away to collect myself. Quickster and the others followed me.

"But, young Earth child, we must find your friend. The area around our great city is treacherous. That unibear is not the only creature out here. If we do not find your friend, he will surely perish before night fall," Quickster said with fear in his voice.

"Why should I help that coward after he left us to die?" I spat. "If it weren't for you, I would've died and just become a shrieking echo."

Lee tried to reason with me and said, "Xolten, I know you're not on good terms with Barry, but we can't let him die, man. He our friend."

"But he left me to die!" I replied.

"But we can't leave him behind or he will face the same fate that almost took you. Think about that. Barry might not be a perfect person, but he doesn't deserve to die like that, "Lee said sternly.

I mulled it over but was not convinced.

"Xolten, I'm gonna give you the choice to either come with us to find Barry or to stay here and wait for us," Lee said.

I did not know what to choose. I had much anger toward Barry for being such a coward. How could I just put all that anger aside? But Lee and the others were right and I swallowed my pride and agreed to help find Barry.

"Excellent choice, earthling. Let's find safety before nightfall, which will occur in two snis," Quickster said happily.

"What are snis?" Sergio asked as we walked along.

"They are like hours on your Earth," Quickster replied.

"Oh, so we have two hours to find him?" Acery replied.

"Exactly," Quickster replied.

"Guys?" a voice from behind us called our attention as we turned around.

There was that cowardly Barry sheepishly coming up to us. As he neared, my anger mounted until I could not control myself. I grabbed Barry and hit him as hard I could. My bone felt like it shattered as I pummeled Barry to the ground. The others came running and tried to restrain me from hurting Barry more, but I kept breaking free and punching Barry.

"You coward!" I yelled angrily at the cowering Barry.

"Xolten, I'm sorry. I was really scared."

"That means nothing to me!"

"Xolten, please forgive me!"

"When we get back to Earth, you and I are done!"

I broke away from the group and started walking on my own.

"Earthling?" I heard Quickster call out to me.

"What do you want?" I asked as I tried to be polite to this helpful being.

"We can go to my city from here. There you can find the answers you seek. I suggest you agree, for we shall surely perish out here," he said.

I paused a moment trying to think of what to do. I wanted to punch Barry again, but I could not let my anger cloud my mind and decision making abilities. I had to go to follow Quickster's advice for the benefit of our whole group.

Trying to sound calm and relaxed, I agreed. Quickster seemed happy as he took the lead, guiding us through the thick brush. We walked in silence for what seemed like forever.

Finally, we arrived at his city, which was full of life. Everywhere we looked seemed to be sparkling with energy. I was awestruck and forgot my anger and quickened by pace with excitement. We finally arrived at Quickster's house where we all settled in to rest our weary bones.

But our minds were filled with questions.

"What is this place?" Sergio asked.

"Are you an alien?" Citlalie asked.

"Why are there two suns in the sky?" Acery asked.

"How do you know about Earth and us humans?" I asked.

"Can you help us get back to our Earth?" Lee asked.

Quickstarter surveyed the room and made a statement that covered many of our questions as he said, "Our great city is called Quickster-opolis and it is on the planet Quicktopia. I am part of the race called the micky-do-quicky-dos. I know all about Earth and you humans because it is my job to research it."

"Wait, hold up," I interjected. "You study us?"

"Yes, we do," Quickster said. "We know about the Milky Way Galaxy and the different planets."

We were all so amazed by the advanced knowledge of Quickster's people.

"And our planet has two suns. Lastly, I do not know if I can help you get back to Earth. It is one gillion light years away from here. I do not even know how you got here. All I know is that I was sent to check out an anomaly in the woods, and that is where I found you all."

I was overwhelmed by all this information, but I knew we still needed Quickster's help. I took him aside and told him all about the company that had commissioned the contest for the revolutionary invention. I explained my concept and how the test run had gone haywire. I also told him about the vortex and how we had traveled through a whirlpool in space and arrived on his planet.

Quickster, who also liked the name Tim, pondered everything I had told him and finally said, "I can help."

"Really?" I asked.

"Yes, we need to recreate this whirlpool on our planet."

"That makes sense."

"But we cannot."

"Why?"

"We are a very advanced race, but we do not have a single piece of technology in the city."

Everyone gasped in shock.

"Yes, I am sorry, my friends," the crestfallen Quickster said.

I did not want to give up and I said, "But there has to be some tech here?"

"The only thing I know about is all the way in another far away city," Quickster said sadly.

Even though this was no great news, it still offered a glimmer of hope and I asked if Quickster would consider taking us there.

"No, I can't because that would require the city leader's permission and his willingness to reveal the city's location," Quickster solemnly added.

"We must speak to the leader and convince him to help us," I said in a resolute tone.

Quickster did not seem convinced, but I could tell he did want to help us as he agreed to represent us to his city's leader.

As we left Quickster's house, the city's nightlife brightened up the dark sky. All the families and friends clearly enjoyed this city that was illuminated with life and my crew and I found ourselves distracted by every little thing.

I started to wonder if I really did want to return to boring old Earth. Quickster's city had all types of incredible animals. I was especially drawn to one called the infinity bird. I saw a life that was so peaceful and charming that I wondered if they ever had strife or war.

We finally arrived at the city's grand citadel where a shadow from the darkness shouted out, "Halt! Who goes there?"

Quickster explained to the imposing guard that he had brought guests to speak to the leader.

I quickly realized that Quickster and the guard whom he called Robert knew each other. This made me hope that we would actually get to meet the leader.

"Nope, I am sorry. The leader has gone to sleep. Please come back tomorrow," Robert said sternly.

Quickster just seemed to accept this as fact and turned to leave.

"Damn it!" I screamed angrily.

Quickster was caught off guard, but said, "I'm sorry, my friends. Tomorrow we can talk to the leader."

"Okay, but we need a place to stay the night," I said shivering as we walked down the path.

"How about my place?" Quickster said.

Everyone agreed that that was certainly the best option.

As we walked to Quickster's house I couldn't help but think about everything that happened. I wondered whether or not we would really make it back home and how I would ever repair my relationship with my brother.

At last, we had arrived at Quickster's house. We were all exhausted and immediately settled in to sleep next to the fireplace. I settled in myself and closed my eyes to sleep, but I was quickly jarred awake by someone sobbing. Acery was sobbing while Citlalie tried to comfort her. Barry, Lee, and Sergio all just lay in their makeshift beds staring at the ceiling.

"Guys, is everything okay?" I asked them all.

"Well, no," Citlalie said.

"F*ck, no!" Acery cried as she continued to bawl her eyes out.

"What do you think?" Sergio said sarcastically.

"What a stupid question!" Barry exclaimed.

Lee looked at me and just shook his head.

"Look, I know things don't look good right now, but we can do this. We've had a couple of setbacks in trying to get home, but I'm sure tomorrow we will all be on our way back to Earth," I said to try and comfort and rally them.

"Don't give us that bullsh*t, oh fearless leader. You're the one who brought us here in the first place. If it wasn't for you and your stupid invention, we would all be back home happy as little clams. But no, you had to build that machine and get us trapped here!" Barry screamed angrily.

"Yeah," the others said in unison.

"I'm sorry I got you trapped here. It wasn't my fault that the machine malfunctioned. I'm trying to right this situation as fast as I can," I answered back.

"That's not good enough. This all your fault, Xolten," Barry exclaimed.

Of course, that no good bastard Barry was trying to get up in my face and turn everyone against me. Something inside me snapped and I pounced on Barry. I hit him in the face as hard I could. He hit me back while the girls watched in horror. Sergio and Lee tried to break up our fight, but we were so angry it was impossible to get between us. I could feel the anger radiating from Barry.

Finally, they separated us and restrained each of us, who still had fight in us. Our faces were bruised and bloody. While the girls calmed Barry down, Lee and Sergio took me outside to cool off.

"Hey, what's your problem, Xolten?" Lee said sternly.

"Yeah?" Sergio added.

"Nothing," I replied in frustration.

"Yeah, well, it doesn't seem that way to us. You just got into it with Barry. He's one of your best friends," Lee said angrily.

"It's just that he made me snap," I screamed out into the dark night as I turned away from them to hide my tears of anger.

"Barry left me to die and now that coward acts like this whole situation is my fault," I countered.

Lee put his arm around me to comfort and calm me.

"I'm sure Barry was just as afraid as everyone when the bear creature attacked you and I'm sure he didn't really mean what he said inside," Sergio added.

"Give it some time," they both said together.

I took a few deep breaths and decided they were right. I went back in to try to apologize to Barry only to be met with complete resistance from him. He seemed even angrier than before and just sulked off by himself to find somewhere else in the house to sleep. I threw my hands up in the air in frustration and decided that we would both sleep on it and start fresh in the morning.

But the morning brought more troubles — everyone was gone and there was a note on the table in the living room:

Xolten, we went to go see the Quickster leader. We'll be back soon. Citlalie.

I got up quickly and started out the door for the citadel where the Quickster leader resided. I tried to remember the directions, but quickly got lost in the city streets. A local was kind enough to give me directions.

Again, I was distracted by the many interesting sights in the city, including even more exotic animals and fierce weapons.

I arrived at the citadel just as the others were exiting.

I raced over to them and asked, "Guys, what happened? What did the Quickster leader tell you? I'm sorry I woke up late."

Lee looked forlorn and said, "The leader told us that we're stuck here because the other city is super far away. And the only way to get there is to go through the Trail of Death, which is nearly impossible to survive."

"We're stuck here forever," Barry replied sarcastically.

I was tired of Barry's crap and I screamed, "You know what, Barry? F*ck you! You are nothing but a negative pain in the butt. You just whine and attack me when I'm trying my hardest to get us back to Earth. Why don't you leave? We would be better off without you, okay? Go! You contribute nothing! Leave!"

I balled up my fists to fight.

"I wish you had died in that bear attack," Barry sneered as he turned to leave.

The others implored him to stay with the group, but to no avail.

Everything seemed impossible as our group was splintering and we had no way to cross the Trail of Death to get the technology in the other city.

How would we ever get home? I wanted to see my family.

Everything seemed so hopeless and I fell to my knees sobbing.

"I don't know what to do, everyone. I'm so sorry I brought you here. Just leave me to rot here. Go join Barry and form your own team," I sputtered.

The others gazed at me in shock, as they had never heard me give up on anything before. They all began to comfort me.

"It's fine," Lee said.

"It's not all your fault," Citlalie added.

"Yeah, we helped you build the machine," Acery said.

"Dude, stop crying. We'll get through this. We just have to put our brains together," Sergio said.

The whole time Quickster had been listening attentively to our discussion and chimed in, "I might have a plan. We can get to the other city Quicksteropilious if we leave at daybreak and travel through the Trail of Death. We must make it in less than a day in order to survive."

"How are we gonna do that and why can't we go by night when it's cooler?" I asked Quickster.

He did not answer my question directly, but continued and added, "We can take the leader's vehicle."

"Wait, you said you don't have any technology here," I said, puzzled.

"We don't, but the leader and the other city do," Quickster replied.

"But won't that be stealing and why can't we go by night?" I pressed Quickster again.

"It will be considered stealing and the dangers at night are much more formidable than the heat of the day. No one has ever survived a night journey and no one even knows exactly what types of creatures exist in that wasteland," Quickster solemnly added.

I shook my head to try and wrap my mind around everything that had to happen for us to even try to get back home.

"So, we need to steal the leader's transportation, survive the Trail of Death, get the technology, built our portal, and survive the journey home?" I asked Quickster and the group.

We all looked at each other silently.

I took a deep breath and said, "Okay, let's do it."

"What? Are you crazy?" the others screamed.

"It's our only hope," I said looking at them all.

"But but..." Acery tried to say something to figure out a safer way to accomplish our goal.

"No buts. We have to wake early, steal the car, pass through the checkpoints out to the Trail of Death, and get that technology," I said with resolve.

"We don't know about this. And what about Barry?" Lee asked.

"Too bad for him," I said angrily.

"Okay, we should plan this tonight," Quickster said.

"And eat!" Sergio added.

We proceeded to make plans of how we were going to do this. We also got different supplies and food. We changed our clothes to blend in more with our surroundings. After we had tossed our raggedy clothes, we all settled in to sleep.

The next morning, we woke up extremely early and all walked out of Quickster's house to see that the city was a barren wasteland.

"What happened?" Citlalie cried, as the once bustling city seemed like a ghost town.

We had no time to spare or to figure out what had happened. So, we all made our way to the leader's citadel. We cautiously made our way inside the fortress, which had seemed so massive from outside, but was actually quite small inside. We searched everywhere for the vehicle transporter that Quickster had told us about. Finally, I found a gargantuan car that looked like a monster.

"How do we start it?" I whispered to Quickster.

"You don't," he replied.

Although we had whispered, there was an unexpected echo that amplified our sounds.

"We must hurry!" Quickster said as he pushed us all into the vehicle.

The car roared to life.

"I can help you navigate from the car's computer," Quickster said.

"Anywhere, but here!" I cried.

The car took off as fast as a bullet busting through the wall of the citadel.

"We made it!" I screamed in joy.

"Yes, but that is just the beginning," Quickster said as he drove us away and started to give us lessons in how to operate the car.

He explained that the car was more like what we would think of as a tank with a computer. The most important thing was that nothing captured the car while we were in the Trail of Death. Quickster programmed the computer with the coordinates of the distant city.

As the car drove us out of the city, I began to beam with joy and I felt we were making tangible progress in our plan to return to Earth.

Chapter 3: *WHAT HAVE I DONE?*

"We are here!" Quickster said with a flourish as the car came to a screeching halt.

I got out of the car to stretch my legs and see this infamous Trail of Death. As I surveyed the area, I could not help but wonder what had happened to Barry. But my mind was quickly distracted by Acery and Sergio. I listened to their chatter, but in reality I was lost in thought over the loss of my friendship with Barry.

Even though I was angry at him for abandoning me and for being so negative, we had been friends for years.

"Okay," Quickster called us together around a map. "We have to very careful. I brought this timekeeper to keep us on schedule. The car should be able to make it back and forth two times before nighttime. It isn't even morning yet, so we should have all the time we need. Any questions?"

Citlali's arm shot up and Quickster nodded to her.

"Your timekeeper is called a watch on Earth," she said as she chuckled.

"Okay, anything else?" the confused Quickster continued as the sun rose behind him. "Huh? Who's that? No! It could not be."

We all turned to see who Quickster was looking at and found our lost comrade Barry had made his own journey to meet us.

Barry was all business and just acted like nothing had happened. We all followed along because our task was already tough enough. We got in the car and told it to take through the Trail of Death. At first, the car seemed to disbelieve our directions. Maybe no one had ever taken it through such a perilous region. But finally, the car zoomed off in the right direction.

Strangely enough, we ended up laughing at the whole forbidding name of Trail of Death because there were no real threats that we saw. We noticed one cliff off to the east and a few carnivorous animals hunting their prey. But that was it.

It only took us a few hours to cross the Trail of Death. It was a cakewalk. When we arrived at the city, I was amazed at the integration of technology within nearly every aspect of the people's lives. They used robots that were more like living machines with minds of their own. I tried not to even blink so that I could absorb everything that I saw in this world of marvels.

"Okay," Quickster said sternly. "Don't lollygag. Just get the parts you need to recreate the machine that brought you here. We do not have time to mess around. We need to leave in one hour or we cannot make it back through the Trail of Death. I will stay here with the car."

We all took his advice to heart and set off into the city. We walked for what felt like forever. This city was full with life, just like the other one. But it felt very different because I could always feel people staring at me.

I decided to focus on the task at hand and pulled out the list. We needed a laser, laser platform, shrinking mechanism, and some other parts. Time was running out and we found almost everything, except the laser.

I began to panic until Acery shouted out in joy as she found the very type of laser we needed.

We all beamed with happiness as we hurried back to Quickster. The suns were setting and nightfall was coming. We began to run to the car to beat the darkness. We started to get lost in the market crowds until we heard Quickster's voice calling us to him.

We were all relieved, but Quickster frowned and said, "It took you guys so long! I do not know if we can make it back safely now!"

"Why don't we wait it out and go in the morning?" I said.

"No, we have to return to the citadel. We might have just enough time," Quickster said as he made an impulsive decision to speed through the Trail of Death.

Before we could say anything, Quickster hit the gas as hard as he could. I turned to see the two suns setting behind us. Quickster's intensity made me more and more fearful of what awaited us in the Trail of Death.

As we ventured away from the city lights, a deep darkness enveloped our car and we could barely see the road in front of us and we had to drive incredibly slowly. I thought about us losing our way and careening off the cliff.

Suddenly, I heard a loud roar come from some type of animal. My stomach turned inside out. I could tell the others were afraid as well. Then something started banging on the car with a ferocious intensity.

"Hang on!" Quickster screamed and he revved the engine to try and outrun the unseen beast.

I tried to remain calm, but all my systems were on go and we were propelled blindly into the night.

Quickster shouted, "Everyone, hold on! We are going to crash! We are gonna have to fight for our lives. Grab whatever weapons you can find!"

"Oh god!" Lee screamed.

"F*ck me!" Sergio screamed.

"I don't wanna die!" Acery yelled.

"Jesus!" Citlalie cried out.

"I love you guys. Just know that!" I screamed as we hit a tree and spun out of control and crash-landed upside down near the edge of the cliff.

My vision blurred and my ears rang. I dragged my body out of the smashed up car and tried to get my bearings.

What was going to happen next?

I felt Acery stand up next to me while I tried to wake Quickster and the others who slowly roused and pulled themselves from the wreckage. The car's headlights illuminated the surrounding area.

But we knew we were not alone. The ringing in my ears subsided only to be replaced by the barbaric roars of the desert beasts. The next thing I knew, one had pounced on the shattered front windshield and smashed what was left of it.

"F*ck, I'm not going out like this!" Quickster said in an unusual use of profanity that made us all realize that it was on.

He kept a wary eye on the snarling beast and went to the car's trunk to get out a handful of rifles.

"Have any of you ever fired one of these?" he shouted as more beasts were thudding towards us.

"Hell, no!" we all replied.

"Well, right now would be a good time to learn!" he said handing us each a rifle.

"But I can't kill a living being!" Acery cried.

"It's kill or be killed!" Quickster shouted just as he shot out the brains of one of the beasts.

They were approaching in legions with their tall, lanky bodies. Their red eyes and razor sharp teeth hungered for our flesh that they wanted to shred with their talons.

"Ready to fight?" Quickster yelled as he shot bullets into a few creatures.

I did not get into any philosophical debates and just picked up a rifle and started shooting at those carnivorous bastards. The recoil nearly broke my shoulder and knocked me off my feet, but I kept firing away.

During the haze of battle, a shadow jumped onto the car and killed two of these creatures. It looked like some type of superhuman. What could it be? In a flash of gunpowder, I saw that it was Barry.

His clothes were in tatters and were soaked with blood from his wounds. He persevered and slaughtered beast after beast. Even though we had had such a hard past, my inner heart cheered him on.

Suddenly, one king-like beast sunk a claw right into Barry's chest and ripped through his body, nearly cutting Barry in half.

I let out a piercing cry as I tried to kill it. Barry fell from his perch on the car hood and the terrific beast headed straight towards me. I was frozen in fear as the beast barreled towards me.

BANG! BANG!

The huge beast slowed his run as his knees buckled and he collapsed on the ground. Behind him, I saw the severely injured Barry standing with the rifle trained on the beast's back.

I ran to Barry's aid.

"Hey, Barry! You still with me?" I asked as I held his head up.

"Yeah," he weakly said as he gasped for air.

The others continued to battle and tried to protect Barry from further harm.

"There's too many!" Lee screamed.

"I think this is the last wave," Sergio screamed back.

"I hope so," Quickster yelled.

"I don't wanna kill them anymore," Acery cried out and she dropped her gun.

Citlalie yelled, "I'm out of ammo!"

"Is Barry okay?" Quickster asked, running to me and Barry.

"No, he's not!" I yelled in frustration.

I knew I had to let Barry go and rejoin the battle if I ever wanted any of us to get out of this alive. I raged with fury as I shot beast after beast. I whacked their dying bodies with the butt of my gun. I pummeled them with my bare hands until the whole area around the car looked like a bloodbath.

The beasts were starting to realize that their dinner was too hard to catch and were retreating. But my adrenaline was on fire. My brother Lee came closer to me and put his hand on my shoulder. I was still in the throes of battle and I grabbed his hand and pushed him away.

"Xolten, calm down. It's okay. It's your brother, Lee," he said to me.

But my eyes saw red and I threw a punch at him. He ducked but lost his footing and stumbled to the ground. All this pent up anger raced through my veins and I tackled him and pinned him to the ground. We wrestled and pummeled each other until we broke apart and, to my horror, Lee fell backwards off the cliff.

I was stunned into shocked silence.

"Xolten, you..." Sergio stammered in disbelief.

"Oh, my God!" Citlalie cried.

"What have you done?" Acery shouted out as she fell to her knees to peer over the side of the cliff.

"He's not dead," I frantically started repeating. "I didn't kill him. He's okay. He'll just climb back up the cliff side."

"He's gone and it's all your fault!" Sergio said.

"Shut up! Shut up! No, he's not. It wasn't my fault."

They all started to weep. And my shoulders began to heave in deep pain as the enormity of what I had done in a flash of anger. I had killed my own brother. I looked to the cliff as my only salvation and started to run to rejoin Lee. The others saw my intentions and tackled me to the ground

"You have to live with what you did!" Acery shouted in my ear.

Howls of anger came from my own inner beast as I shouted, "I'm a monster! I'm a terrible human being!"

Quickster did not know what to do with everything that was happening. He called us over to Barry's crumpled form on the ground. He was clearly mortally injured.

I could not handle all this death and begged Quickster to use his special medicine that he had used to heal me from my bear creature attack.

"I'm sorry, but his injuries are too severe. Even the most potent medicine from any planet could not save Barry," Quickster solemnly replied.

I was devastated and cried out, "First my brother Lee and now my best friend Barry. Barry, I'm so sorry for everything I said to you. You saved me tonight. You were so brave and selfless."

I bawled harder than I ever had in my life.

Barry looked at me with the eyes of one who is already seeing through to the other side as he said, "Xolten, life is so complicated. But you gave me the best adventure of my life and my decision to protect all of you was the best thing I've ever done. I know I'm not going to make it back to Quicksteropolis or to my family on Earth. But I'm happy to rest in peace here on this planet."

Everyone came together and held onto Barry as he breathed his last breaths.

We were all lost in tears, but Sergio pulled himself together and asked Quickster about the plan.

"The suns are rising, so we can go through the rest of the Trail of Death and finish the mission," Quickster said with confidence.

"Let's do it," I said wiping the tears from my eyes.

"Let's just stay here on this planet," the girls argued.

"Why?" I asked.

"What are we gonna tell your all our parents about Lee and Barry?" Acery said.

I just shook my head because I did not have the answer, but we finally all agreed to still try to find a way home. We would know what to say when we got back to Earth.

We left the car in the desert and walked the rest of way back to Quickster's house where we quickly reassembled the machine that had brought us so much sorrow.

When I had started this whole project, I had envisioned becoming a great helper to humanity. Instead, I had killed my brother and contributed to the death of my best friend. My first steps back on Earth were filled with sorrow and bitterness.

We looked at the clock in the old warehouse and saw that we had only been gone for half an hour, half an hour that cost two people their lives.

Two months passed and Barry and Lee just became another set of statistics for missing high school students in Los Angeles. We had funerals for them, but our families never really recovered their joy.

Guilt became my soul companion as I became increasingly antisocial.

I could hear my teachers whisper that I had had so much promise.

It was safe to say that the whole trajectory of our lives had been

altered and nothing would ever be the same again. I became a ghost

of myself as I realized that I had killed three people out there in the

Trail of Death. Sometimes I would bitterly laugh to myself at just

how apropos that stupid name ended up being. The guilt haunted me

like a specter as I lived out the rest of my days as a recluse watching

the world pass by my window.

22

Test Subject

By

Leovardo Morales

"Alan Meza, male, eighteen years of age, 175 pounds, 6'3", brown hair, light brown eyes, very athletic. Best Use: Human Testing," an unseen voice announced.

"Wow, that was one weird dream," I thought as I shook myself awake.

I then proceeded to reach for my phone and went on the ifunny site to see what had been recently posted.

I am Alan Walker, by the way, and that description fit me to a tee. I am in fact 175 pounds with brown hair and light brown eyes. I love to play soccer, whether on an actual team or just with friends.

But I do not feel that my best use is really for "Human testing," whatever that would entail.

Anyway, it is almost always nice here in South Central, California. Yes, I know it is not the best place to live, but it is by far not the worst. The streets are somewhat clean but occasionally you will see a mattress, couch, or dead animal on the side of the road.

Both my parents came from Mexico for a better life, which included me attending Alain Leroy Locke High School. Well, I used to, until I graduated last week. I would have liked to have had a big graduation party, but I'm broke. I also don't have many friends. It's not that I am weird or anything; it's just that I like to be by myself sometimes — okay, a lot of the time.

I am also not the smartest man alive, but I would say I am average. I graduated with a mix of A's, B's, and C's. I probably could have done better if I was not such a huge procrastinator. I am so good at procrastinating that I can even procrastinate going to sleep. I often spend hours on my computer to the point of exhaustion. But when I lie down to sleep, I will start searching on my phone for that last little tidbit of fun before I sleep. This can last for hours. And I can see the

dawn starting before I have even closed my eyes.

Well enough about me, let's get back to the real story.

I had just finished watching all the features on ifunny and I was

dying laughing. I got out of bed and walked the short distance to the

kitchen where I saw my dad. My dad is 5'11" and weighs 210

pounds. He also has the same hair and eye color as I do. He was

already up and eating some chocolate donuts at the table.

"Finally! You're up. It's already two-thirty," he said.

"School's finished. I can wake up whenever I want to," I said.

He just looked at me and laughed. I was going to ask him to pass

me a donut, but then we heard an ear-piercing explosion. My dad told

me to wait inside while he ran outside to check what had happened.

My ears were ringing from the explosion and I did not hear his

instruction. I ran outside and was shocked at what I saw.

To my left, the city looked normal style. But the city on the right

was engulfed in flames. A mob was throwing Molotov cocktails into

a house to try to get the people inside to come out into the street.

I saw one person rush out of the inferno only to be pummeled and knocked unconscious by the angry crowd who then threw the limp body into a van that sped away. I saw that there were about twenty vans parked in a line.

My dad turned to me, grabbed my shoulders, and shouted, "Go inside and get the gun from the safe!"

I ran into the house to get the gun, but as I opened the safe I saw someone out of the corner of my eye. It was a skinny kid I did not know who looked around fifteen. When he noticed me, he lunged forward to tackle me. I dodged his attack and he ran head first into the wall and knocked himself out. I expected red blood to pour out of his fractured nose, but green goo leaked out of his nose.

Then a tiny, human-like creature with blue skin came out of his nose. The alien tried to escape, but I caught him before he could run through a small hole in the wall. I had a lot of questions to ask him and I wanted answers. But before I could ask him anything, he grabbed his head and twisted and broke his own neck.

I was so confused. I just ignored everything that had just happened and ran back outside to find my dad, except he was not there. I screamed out his name but there was only the sound of fire, explosions, and other people screaming. Then, I saw an enormously tall and fat man dragging his unconscious body to a van that was parked in front of my neighbor's house.

I couldn't move because I was in shock. Then I heard the enormous guy say that my dad was perfect. He threw my dad into the back of the van and turned to look at me. He tried to run after me, but I easily out ran him. Honestly if it was not such a frightening scenario, I would have been laughing at the image of this beast lumbering after me.

Anyway, I ran as fast as I could in the opposite direction, but apparently we were the last block to be hit by this alien invasion.

"Man," I thought. "If only I could have watched the news, then maybe there would have been some hint that this was about to happen. We could have left before everything happened."

I kept running until I saw a mechanic shop where I stopped. I thought that there might be a car parked in the garage. The lock holding the door down was damaged so just one swift kick broke it. I opened up the door and hoped for a Mustang or some other fast, cool getaway vehicle.

There was only a Prius — a pink, dented Prius with no hood.

I opened the door and luckily the keys were on the floor. I turned the car on and the engine sounded horrible. The only good thing about the car was that you could actually drive it.

I drove without really knowing where to go. Everywhere was on fire. Then I hit a guy who was walking on the street. At first I was horrified because I thought I had hit a person. But then I saw the green goo seeping out of his ears.

As I went to get back into my car, I noticed two white vans parked nearby. I drove off as quickly as I could and hoped that they would not follow me. I turned my head to look back and realized the two vans were following me. I accelerated and raced through the empty streets. I thought that the aliens must have removed all the cars from the streets in order to make room for their vans.

I tried to outrun the vans, but the Prius was a piece of junk. They were catching up to me, and the Prius just would not go any faster. One of the vans hit me on the back right corner of my car. It spun out and then flipped to land upside down. My face was covered in blood and I could not move. My ribs hurt every time I moved and my nose was killing me.

The door opened, and I was dragged out of the crushed car by a different fat guy. I laughed thinking about the earlier guy, but then everything went dark. When I came to, I realized that I was locked in a very small room that could just fit a twin-size bed with enough room for a toilet. I stared at the cell door that had no handle but did have a small, rectangle cut out that was at eye level.

I peered through the cut out to try and understand my surroundings and to plan my escape. Suddenly, a pair of eyes randomly popped up from the other side. I jumped back in fear and knocked my ribs into the wall. The pain was like fire.

"Ha!" said a female voice from the other side. "You should have stayed on your bed. You fractured all of your ribs on the right side. You also broke your nose. You will have one month to recover before we see what category you fall into. I will bring you food for the next month until you get better. Bye."

"Wait. What do you mean by category?" I asked.

"You'll find out eventually" she called over her shoulder as she left.

I was so confused I didn't know what to think anymore. So, I fell asleep.

The girl, who was around 5'8" and a buck twenty, kept true to her word and brought me food for the next month. When the month was almost over, the girl told me something I did not expect.

On the last day of the month, she said, "My name is Jenny. I want to help you escape from this place. I am not under control of those little alien things. I killed the one that was supposed to control me and just acted like I was one of them. I need a little time to come up with a plan to escape."

"Why are you helping me? There are plenty of other people in this place. Why not help them? Why me?" I asked.

"I had a dream before they captured me," she said. "You were in my dream. You are the key to defeating the aliens and will save all of us."

"But that can't be possible. I am just an ordinary guy. There is nothing special about me. And I can't leave this place without my father. He was captured and I know he is somewhere in here. I can feel it."

"There is something very special about you. You probably don't see it, and honestly I don't see it either. But you were in my dream and I feel like some type of force was trying to send me a message. I will help you find your father. Do you have any pictures of him, by chance?"

"Yes, I do," I said and reached into my wallet to show her a picture of my mom, dad, and myself.

"Are you also looking for your mom? Did she get captured and brought here?"

"No, she passed away last year from cancer."

"Oh, I'm sorry to hear that. But wait; is this guy in the picture your dad?"

"Yes. Why?"

She mumbled to herself, but I could still hear her saying that something was going to be harder than expected but that she needed to keep that in mind.

"Is my dad ok?" I asked, with worry.

"Yeah, he's fine, but I don't think you're gonna like where he is at. But we need to deal with that later. I'll break you out of whatever category you land in and then we'll go save your dad."

"Ok, I guess."

What choice did I have and what did it mean "to land in a category?"

With that, she left with a swish of her long, black hair and I tried to get some sleep. I woke up to a very large man pulling me out of bed and dragging me on the floor to another room that had a bed with restraints on it. I did not like the look of this and I liked it even less when I felt him strapping me into those restraints. I could barely move as I watched him lumber away.

Then another man dressed in a black suit walked in with an air of importance about him. Other beings followed behind him, but they wore regular shirts and jeans.

The man in black began to address me and terrify me as he said, "Alan Meza, male, 18 years of age, 175 pounds, 6'3", brown hair, light brown eyes, very athletic. Best Use: Human Testing."

I began to scream and writhe around on the bed. But it was useless as the restraints held me tight. The man just looked at me and laughed as he waited for me to calm down.

He continued, "There are three categories for humans, including sweepers who gather more humans, deliverers who organize food, and entertainers who perform tests on the humans. We all debated about the name of the final category, some wanted to name it the "fun category" because those in that category should enjoy their work. This involves a mixture of skill, patience, and creativity in torturing the subject as much as possible and allowing death at the decided moment. Then, we move on to the next person."

I struggled on the bed and shouted, "Why are you doing this? What is the purpose of all this?"

The man in black calmly responded, "I'm glad you asked. Our species needs pain to survive. When you feel pain, it releases a chemical called zynom that we need to survive. It's basically oxygen to us. We can survive inside a human for twenty-four hours without it, but then we need to find and inhale more zynom."

After that, he started to torture me. He told me that he was going to start easy and that I would have two weeks to recover until the next session. He used a small hammer to swiftly break my nose and all my ribs on my left side.

I then spent the next week and six days resting my bones. I could barely move as the pain was excruciating. On the last day of my break, Jenny arrived with a twinkle in her warm, brown eyes.

"Come on, we need to get out of here. We are going to get your dad so we can escape now. I've found the alien's weakness," she said as she opened my cell door.

I ran behind her and followed her every move until we reached a huge door where she stopped.

"Your dad is in there. But I have to warn you that he's not exactly the dad that you remember. The leader of the aliens took over your dad's body as his own. I hate to have to tell you that, we have a chance to take out the aliens by taking out their leader," she said.

I knew exactly why she was being so serious as I said, "But that would include killing my dad, right?"

"I'm sorry, but this is bigger than just the three of us. The aliens are dependent on their leader and will die off without his centralizing life force here on Earth. The remaining ones will return to their home planet to reinvigorate their beings."

"How do you know that killing the leader will lead to the alien's leaving? He's just one being? Won't they just find another leader?"

"No, there's a special connection between the leader and the other aliens who follow all his orders. If the leader dies, the others will go insane because they can't understand how to make decisions on their own."

"How can I trust you? How do I know you're really still human? How can I know that sacrificing my father's life will really lead to saving humanity?

"I'll tell you later. Trust me, it will work."

She pumped herself up to storm the room, but I stopped her because I had to ask her one vital question. "You never told me their weakness."

She shook her head in a way that I knew that she would not answer me and just said, "Hit them in the head as hard as you can."

We burst into the room to find twelve burly men aiming guns at us.

"But how?" Jenny said in devastated confusion.

"I just had a feeling," I heard my dad's voice say, as the alien using his body stepped out from behind the row of bodyguards. "One of my men overheard you talking. Maybe you should try to whisper lower next time? Oh, wait. There isn't going to be a next time. Men, take them outside and kill them in front of everyone. Let this be a warning to anyone who wants to try to disobey orders."

Jenny shrieked and I shouted as they quickly handcuffed us and started marching us towards the common area to be executed. My life flashed before my eyes — I had barely accomplished any of the things I wanted to do in my life. I wanted to go skydiving and travel the world. I turned to look at Jenny and was shocked to see her smiling.

She looked calm as could be and she turned to me and mouthed the words, "Three...Two...One."

Suddenly, a group of kids jumped out of nowhere and attacked the bodyguards with a range of weapons like hammers and bats. The guards fell to the ground as green goo oozed out of their wounds.

Jenny surveyed the scene with joy and said to me, "You always have to have a back-up plan just in case."

Then we both started laughing at the absurdity of the entire situation. I grabbed one of the bats and we ran back inside to find the supreme leader who was using my father's body.

This powerful man looked frightened when he saw us approaching and cowered and said, "Don't get any closer. I'm inside your dad's head. I can kill h…"

Before that little minion could finish the sentence, I swung the baseball bat at the back of my dad's head. It was a calculated move as I hit him softly enough to prevent brain damage to my dad but hard enough to send that alien flying out of his nose.

The little alien hit the ground and went splat. Other guards arrived just in time to see the alien leader writhing in his death throes. The other aliens descended from the human guards' noses and slinked away as the guards crumpled to the ground.

"Jenny, how did you know the plan would work?" I asked.

"I had learned from another alien that most of them were tired of living the life of colonizing planets and torturing the inhabitants. They wanted to go home."

A feeling of peace came over me as I realized that I would not be facing another round of torture, until suddenly I remembered that we needed to bring my dad back to consciousness.

We picked up my dad who struggled to walk and seemed to mumble words to me asking where we were. I had no idea myself.

Jenny and I supported him by carrying him under each arm as we found the large door that seemed to lead to an outer world. When we opened the door, the sun blinded us and we had to use our free hands to cover our eyes. When I could see, I realized that we were in a desert and had been held in a military bunker. I surmised that we were in Nevada in Area 51.

I laughed as I realized that the aliens had been holding us prisoner in the very place that we had held other aliens prisoner — talk about who is in the fish bowl now?

I turned to Jenny and asked, "Where are you going from here?"

"I am going to go look for my parents. They were not captured and I have to go find them."

"Ok, I wish you good luck in finding then."

"Thanks" She said. "So, I guess this is goodbye."

"I guess it is," I said. "I'm sorry. I'm not really good at goodbyes. I tend to make them awkward."

"High five, then?" she said as we did a lame high-five. "Here's my number so we can stay in touch."

"Goodbye," I said.

And, with that, she set off to find her parents. I dragged my dad into an army jeep that was nearby and drove off.

Epilogue

The government needed help rebuilding human life on planet Earth. We focused our efforts on the West Coast and I led the South Central brigade. We planted food and formed new democracies and tried to fix problems that had long plagued humanity before the alien invasion. I still kept in contact with Jenny and was happy to learn that she had found her parents. We have restarted our education programs and I am now in college and studying computer science. My life is normal, but I have a feeling that there are going to be more alien invasions in the future. I feel that that was only the beginning and that there is more to come.

Made in the USA
Charleston, SC
23 October 2016